Yooooou can...
Yooooou should...
Write Poetry

Good Rhyming

You Can... You Should...
Write Poetry

MARSH CREEK PRESS

Published by Marsh Creek Press,
PO Box 700,
Pocatello, Idaho 83204
Phone 208-232-3535.

ISBN 0-937750-20-4

Also by Don Aslett

Help with Personal Management:

How to Have a 48-Hour Day

How to Handle 1,000 Things at Once

Help for Packrats:

Clutter's Last Stand

Not for Packrats Only

Clutter Free! Finally & Forever

The Office Clutter Cure

How to Clean:

Is There Life After Housework?

Do I Dust or Vacuum First?

Make Your House Do the Housework

Don Aslett's Clean in a Minute

Who Says It's a Woman's Job to Clean?

500 Terrific Ideas for Cleaning Everything

Pet Clean-Up Made Easy

How Do I Clean the Moosehead?

Don Aslett's Stainbuster's Bible

The Cleaning Encyclopedia

Professional Cleaning Books:

Cleaning Up for a Living

The Professional Cleaner's Personal Handbook

How to Upgrade & Motivate Your Cleaning Crews

Construction Cleanup

Painting Without Fainting

Don Aslett's Professional Cleaner's Clip Art

Business Books:

How to be #1 With Your Boss

Everything I Needed to Know About Business
  I Learned in the Barnyard

Speak Up!

TABLE OF CONTENTS

INTRODUCTION

What are my rights, qualifications, my authority or whatever to write about poetry?

The nice big truth about poetry is that no one owns it, no degree qualifies you for it, and there is no one judge of it. That means any person anywhere can write it...has the right to do it.

Like most of you reading this book I just love writing poetry.

Not many people know that. They see my more than two dozen best-selling books, my national cleaning company and corporate activities, and all my public speaking and TV appearances, but few know that my favorite niche of all is verse. I've turned out hundreds of rhymes, one-liners to four-pagers, because I enjoy it immensely. I've used poetry in my own personal life, in about as many different situations as you can imagine. And if that were the only value of verse for you or me, it would be one of the greatest values on earth.

My poems have been productive and fun for me, brought many grins and grimaces from others, and been circulated and read at events all over the country (hopefully not critics' conventions!). I've written volumes of company verse and passed it throughout my companies, welcoming return verses or rebuttals. A goodly part of my sixty years of living has been recorded in poems, and they have been a real addition to my quality of life.

The purpose of this book is to share how and why.

When I taught high school literature classes many years ago, I found that pulling poems out of students was the most exciting part of the class. Now I'd like to pull some poems out of YOU. I hope you will turn to keyboard or tablet too, and spice up your life and the lives of those around you!

—Don Aslett

P. S. Many verses from others, beginners to masters, are quoted and displayed in this book, but I've also used quite a few of my own poems, because I know them and they fit in some of the places where I want to make a point. Being shown how and why someone else did something I want to do has always really helped me. I've never liked the teachers, speakers, and writers who just gather up other people's stuff and present it with their comments and evaluations. Besides folks, this is my book, and what would you do if you were writing a book on how to write poems? Would you use someone else's throughout the book? Not on your life!

**Sure
you have
a message
for
mankind!**

You have feelings no one knows about. You want to be heard and listened to, you have lots of thoughts and ideas and opinions, and you want to record some of your stories and messages too. Few of you actually put your feelings on paper, but you feel the urge to. I am that way, all people are that way, and plenty of us have timidly taken steps to record some of those thoughts and feelings—believe it or not, in verse… yes poetry.

Lots of us have clipped some poems or rhymes and many of us have memorized them, too. We like them. Most people like if not love poetry. Few will admit it, especially the big backhoe operator or the butcher, but they, like you, have some verses, a few lines or so tucked away in secret somewhere or in scribbled notes..

One of my big basic motivations for this book is to get you talented folks out there to just "do it," too—write and use your poems—first for yourself and second for others, family, friends, employees, the cat, whomever you please. This book is meant to convince you to do it, give you some examples and show you how to do it in a common, everyday sort of way. I hope it may be just the catalyst you need to get started writing up those poems you've wanted to write. Or started and never finished.

What you haven't yet written, I know you have it in you to write. What you have written, I encourage you to get out and in use. That is the sole purpose of this book—getting YOUR poems out and into the light of day. Here is some direction, encouragement, and I hope inspiration to do your poem thing… and not be bashful about it.

CHAPTER ONE

How I got hooked on poetry

It was one of the old two-room, rural schoolhouses, with just two teachers. It had a big room (grades 5 to 8) and a little room (grades 1 to 4). I was in the fourth grade, a senior in the little room. Next to my row, which had slightly larger desks, the lowly third graders took up their educational position in one of those old rows of desks all connected together. It was Valentine's Day, not only one of the precious holidays of a country school, but one of the few days we were officially exposed to "poetry."

Man, that was erotic stuff! Some verses on those penny valentines mentioned "heart," and "mine," "cute," and many other risqué phrases in those days of '44. In every package of fifty valentines there were at least two that actually said the forbidden blushing words… "I love you." Many a grade schooler agonized for days over who and if to route those two cards. Most of the messages on the valentines were in some kind of clever rhyme and though we were all familiar with good old Mother Goose—the Hickory, Dickory, Dock and Clock rhymes we all knew by heart—these valentine rhymes were new, hot stuff, tapping our natural human love for verse.

Our teacher, Mrs. Kirkpatrick, sensitive and perceptive even at the advanced age of twenty-seven years, was enthusiastic about verse herself and saw here a great opportunity to further our love for it. And so she instructed us to fold some of that stiff red paper we had in those days and cut out our own homemade valentine. And then (hold your breath), the biggest step in school up to then, we were told to write our

4

own poem inside the valentine! All of us bent to the task, our palms sweating with embarrassment as to which girl or boy we were thinking of. It was almost too much for a nine-year-old.

I can't remember my first poem, but it made the teacher nod approvingly. Was I motivated or what? Longfellow look out when I get to the fifth grade and the big room! One little third grader, super shy, wasn't as prone to the poetic occasion and refused to write. Our teacher despised the words "can't" and "won't" and the more she bullied him, the further his bottom lip protruded. It seemed a sure standoff until Mrs. Kirkpatrick informed him it was a verse or worse situation (a rap with the ruler, the corner, or demotion from the Bluebirds to the Blackbirds).

Finally he wrote.

The teacher, basking in her triumph of getting him to write and now pushing her luck, asked the backward little fellow to stand up and read it. Now writing a poem was one thing, but reading out loud, in front of the whole class, was a bit much. He didn't move, the predictable behavior of a bashful eight-year-old. Teacher power in those days was really something. I can't remember the clincher, but she was victorious again and he rose and read, in clear young voice:

"Roses are red
Violets are blue
I'd rather be flushed down the toilet
Than sit by you!"

The room exploded with admiration and clapping. No one cared about the insult (except the teacher, I guess). But what a rhyme! What a punchline! "Wow!" I thought, that kid can really put it out. I

admired poems and had memorized a few famous ones, but right here next to me a snot-nosed little kid blew us all out of the water, with a truly self-made structure, that rhymed!

For weeks afterward all the kids repeated it—even the big room kids heard about it and learned it. That bashful kid's self-esteem must have quadrupled. It's been more than fifty years since that enlightening day, and I'll bet you every single person that was there, remembers that verse today!

I don't know for sure if it was this third grader's poem, the teacher's approval of my poem, or my mother's always keeping books of good poetry around, but for me poetry held a revered place in my life forever after.

Something put in poetry will be said better and remembered longer than any other kind of communication. It can flex feelings like nothing else, it can latch on to you and stay. Not long ago riding back from Sacramento, California to Idaho (700 miles), I recited "Casey at the Bat," which I memorized fifty years ago. Yet I couldn't remember the script from a TV program I'd appeared on four hours earlier.

After that fourth-grade epiphany, for the next several years of grade school, I was on my own. There was a sprinkle of poetry here and there, but few teachers held it in the same regard as reading, writing, and arithmetic. My 5-7 grade class (of three boys total) had an ex-marine for a teacher who marched us through the regular assignments, but not much, if anything in verse. I can remember Mother reading some us verse and me finding some in library books and sneaking it in when other schoolwork was caught up. But the eighth-grade teacher was a gift from heaven. She was undoubtedly one of the most influential women in my life. Mrs. Rickets was nothing short of an inspired angel, and to know and be taught by her was heaven indeed. She was twice as tough as the ex-marine, but she loved her students and constantly confessed her love of poetry and read and assigned us poems and the rhyme leaves turned green again.

I've saved the choicest spot in my autobiography for Mrs. Rickets. Her view of poetry was that it is the spark and the spice of life, and this is a vision I've never let loose of.

When I moved up to a high school of six hundred students, it was like going from Sawmill City to New York City. I barely survived big new courses like Spanish, algebra, geometry, and sociology, and the English and grammar here was another language. I was sure the teachers took courses in "how to make it difficult for a student to learn." Not a poem all that first year that I remember.

Then my father bought a ranch, a remote ranch to be sure. The nearest neighbor to the west was eighty-five miles, to the north fifteen miles, to the south three miles and about that to the east. The whole high school, my alma mater to be, had forty-two students in all. Not many poetic teachers made it out this far, and the ones we did have kind of skipped the poems when they popped up in Lit. But I had two big things going for me—working with a father eight hours a day who had the magic of encouraging self-esteem and self-confidence in me and my brothers, and the fact that I still loved poems. I'd read every one Mother had in her old trunk of books. In this little school, I was reporter on the school paper, the Devil's Diary, and when I was offered a blank page to fill one day I did a new rendition of "The Night Before Christmas," orienting it to the jocks and the ball team, calling it "The Night Before the Ball Game." Don't worry, I won't lay it all on you here, but this will give you some idea of the flavor of my first big published verse:

'Twas the night before the ball game and all through the dance,
Every creature was stirring, oh how they did prance,
The watches were hung on the boys' arms with care,
In hopes that "the coach" would never be there.

Anyway, the poem set up the arrival of the coach like Santa.

Then what to my wondering eyes should approach,
But that short ugly man known as the "coach."

That wasn't enough, so gave him a couple of more shots in the next stanza:

His eyes how they flashed,
His dimple how awful.
His cheeks were like Pluto's
His nose like a waffle.

When the school paper hit the street with the full version of the stunning poem, it was a smash! It was copied and sent to friends, and coach even sent a copy to his parents and fellow coaches. I learned from this venture that in verse one can call an adult short and ugly and if published to all, you won't get whacked for it.

From then on I started to write poetry, generally little verses to fit a particular situation, while most of the people around me never even imagined themselves doing such silly stuff.

Somewhere around the age of fourteen or fifteen, I remember feeling the impact and sadness that a single poem could bring. About the time we were reading the "The Wreck of the Hesperus" in school, one of my cousins, a little girl of four, was accidentally shot and killed. As death introduced itself in real life, it came alive in the poems too. I remember her parents and my parents grieving over the loss of that beautiful child as I was reading about a mariner taking his daughter to sea and running into a gale so strong, disaster was sure. The old father, doing all he could to save his little girl, tied her to the mast so she couldn't be swept off the deck. The ship went down, and the verse:

Her rattling shrouds, all sheathed
  in ice,
With the masts went by the board;
Like a vessel of glass she strove and
  sank,
Ho! ho! the breakers roared!

At daybreak on the bleak sea beach
A fisherman stood aghast,
To see the form of a maiden fair
Lashed close to a drifting mast.

The salt sea was frozen on her breast,
The salt tears in her eyes;
And he saw her hair, like
  the brown seaweed,
On the billows fall
  and rise.

I read that a hundred times and dreamed about it and lived through that storm with the father and the daughter. Over my life, I've run into other poems too that cut deep into my emotions.

It never occurred to me to write seriously on love or death or the like myself. My debut had been the light touch comedy verse for the occasion and so it was when I entered college. In high school I'd attended several seminars on graphic art and newspaper writing, and done the usual essay writing for composition classes and the like. I'd also started my own cleaning business (at eighteen), then served two years as a missionary in Hawaii. And so when I started at Idaho State University at the seasoned age of twenty-three, I was married, a businessman, and serious about getting an education, not just going to school for a grade or job—those were the last priorities.

Now came the poetry in full-strength doses, along with all kinds of explanations, philosophies, and a history in detail of every poet and most of their works and there was some good, good stuff. But there was also lots of less than good stuff. At that time you wouldn't dare say anything was dull because it was "in the book" that we paid $30.00 for. One time, the only time in my life I can remember being humiliated, an instructor made me get up (Aslett comes early in alphabetical seating) and read a part of "The Canterbury Tales" in the original Old English. It was stupid—I thought so then, and know so now. I read it to the best of my ability in ordinary English and she slapped the desk violently and said, "Read it like it is written, Aslett!"

Here I was a full-grown businessman reading with an odd accent that no one understood or liked. The next year, one of my English teachers made the statement, "If you cannot appreciate Milton, Keats, and Shelley, you aren't an educated person." I labored on their stuff for months and finally accepted that I wasn't an educated man.

Today, now that I'm a best-selling author of more than two dozen books and a seasoned veteran of life, business, and teaching, I have the courage to admit I wouldn't trade half of all those famous "Lit" poems for twelve of Robert Service's.

But the other half of the masters, they are wonderful, their poems lived for me. Maybe the other half lives for some of you. The point is, who defines what makes a master? I say **you,** plain, old you, have the same emotions, passions, even talents they had. And because two hundred years ago when there was much less around to be selected from they made it to the "college course book" to be handed and handed down forever, doesn't mean all the "forever in print" are the masters. We have as good or better a chance today… maybe even you!

Shakespeare was a master. He never goes out of style. He was brilliant, knew life, caught it, and wrote it. Look what Edwin Markham did with "Preparedness." This short verse is one of the ones that guide my life. It says more than most of the best business books and seminars, all in one short jab of verse:

For all your days prepare,
And meet them ever alike;
When you are the anvil bear—
And when you are the hammer strike.
—Edwin Markham

I found this so easy to understand and apply I even began, when I wanted to get a message over to a fellow businessperson, to drop the call and dull letter routine and just jot a verse. One of my vendors that furnished dust mops and door mats for my company, for instance, gouged me on a billing, so I thought I'd serve him a different kind of account questioning than he usually got:

A Janitor's Expenses

My lawyer drives a Lincoln, a Porsche
  transports my CPA
My banker has a Rolls Royce, I see him
  every day!
My chemical supplier has two Cadillacs,
  chauffeured by two ladies
But I get suspicious when my dust mop
  man drives by in his new Mercedes!
  —DA Sun Valley 1969

Going to school full time, raising a family, and being active in community and church activities, scouting, and athletics presented opportunities to use verse again and again. Think of the times we've all been cornered or requested or our turn came to perform, sing, act, be in a talent show, or the like. Seems we always hunt for some old standby poem, song, or skit. By now I found out that **doing your own was easier and generally better**. For years I'd watched Road Shows, locally written plays and lyrics, not copied, but written from scratch to fit the occasion. At least three quarters of the time, they were much, much better than the old worn-out ones. There were homemakers, janitors, teachers, students, even little kids who could put the most darling verse down. So I started doing it, too. When someone asked me and my wife or daughter to perform or participate in the Junior Miss Pageant or the like, we did our own song, verse, or script and we did winners, too. Winners because it was from us, not an equal who just happened to get published.

Living in town all the while I attended college and built my maintenance business (almost eight years), my wife and I now had four little kids, a degree, and a yearning to get back into the country. I found a nice sixty-acre place in some of the most beautiful mountains in the world—Southern Idaho. As soon as we moved onto it, a neighbor, Jimmy Guthrie, asked if he could run some of his cattle on our meadows and hills. He said he'd fence the property and put up gates as necessary. Jimmy was about thirty, looked twelve (he's now sixty, looks twenty). Anyway, he showed up to fence, and since I was a seasoned fencer—I'd fenced at least 3000 acres of cow range since the age of thirteen—I strapped on my tools to help by showing him some new fence moves. But guess what, the guy was a madman! We fenced in a fever, and I was in low gear by comparison. When the fence was done, I was so impressed that nothing seemed good enough to capture the experience. Except (you guessed it) a poem. So I sat down and jotted an ode called "The Mad Fencer of McCammon."

This is an excerpt from the middle of the page-long poem that described the whole process:

I thought he was a madman as he whipped the wire around
He spit the staples in the post before I could turn around.
He carried three buckets filled with ties, boy, he didn't poke
He hooked and tied at such a speed, the pliers began to smoke.

I liked the result and being new in the community, I figured I'd give it a shot and send it in to the paper. They published it. The community loved Jimmy Guthrie and now here was a poem recognizing him (someone right from their home town) as the number one in the world. It didn't hurt my PR as a newcomer, either.

That summer after I graduated from Idaho State, I planned to work full time in the maintenance business. I had a big contract with the Bell System, but a call from a desperate high school principal two days before school opened for the year convinced me I should at least teach some with my degree. Sure that I could keep the business going and teach a year, I accepted, unaware that I was going to teach ENGLISH! Man, I didn't have any idea what an adverb was, never mind a subjective complement or dangling participle, but that was immaterial. I was in. I taught junior and senior English. They did give me a choice of grammar or great writings. Should you wonder which I focused on? This was a rural community that related to cowboys and athletics more than the great poets of the ages. In fact, I don't know if some of the townspeople were even aware that there were great poets.

The students were great, and my business experience of employing hundreds of people prior to teaching gave me a position of confidence. I whipped past the grammar and sentence structure stuff in record time. That was easy because every student knew more than I did (all having had the master English teacher of the world the year before). Into the literature and poetry part we went, with many groans and catcalls from those with the biggest jock butts and longest sideburns. I vowed to myself in preparation for the classes that they would all march time to some rhyme before we were through… and they did. It puzzled a lot of parents to see their big bored teenager come home and hide out in a locked room writing a poem… and proud of it.

The first day in Lit class, I asked the students to take out a piece of paper and write on it a paragraph: 1. telling someone how much they love them, 2. describing how cold it was outside, 3. explaining the wrongness of gossip and ruining someone's good name, and several more of life's difficult situations.

I let them labor the whole hour of class on this and they did labor. They begged not to have to do it, and no one wanted to read their descriptions even after they were written, not even the straight "A" students trying to make a good impression on me.

I waited until fifteen minutes before the class was over and then asked them if they would like to hear how the masters wrote on those same subjects. For that difficult business of telling someone how much you love them, I read Elizabeth Barrett Browning's "How Do I Love Thee."

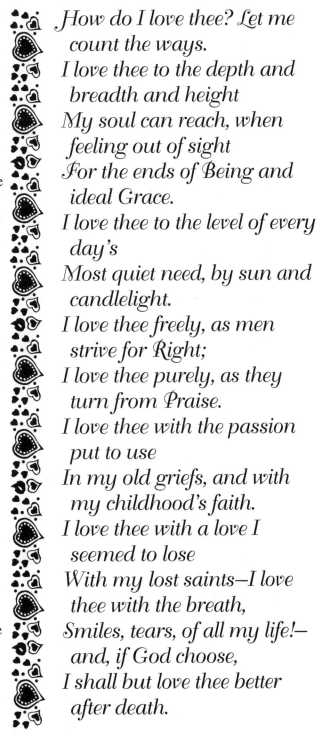

How do I love thee? Let me count the ways.
I love thee to the depth and breadth and height
My soul can reach, when feeling out of sight
For the ends of Being and ideal Grace.
I love thee to the level of every day's
Most quiet need, by sun and candlelight.
I love thee freely, as men strive for Right;
I love thee purely, as they turn from Praise.
I love thee with the passion put to use
In my old griefs, and with my childhood's faith.
I love thee with a love I seemed to lose
With my lost saints—I love thee with the breath,
Smiles, tears, of all my life!—and, if God choose,
I shall but love thee better after death.

For number two, I cranked out a Robert Service verse on the Yukon cold… and heard shivers:

You know what it's like in the
   Yukon wild when it's sixty-nine
   below
When the ice-worms wriggle their
   purple heads through the crust
   of the pale blue snow;
When the pine-trees crack like
   little guns in the silence of the
   wood,
And the icicles hang down like
   tusks under the parka hood;
When the stove-pipe smoke
   breaks sudden off, and the sky
   is weirdly lit,
And the careless feel of a bit of
   steel burns like a red-hot spit.

For a description of the evils of gossip, I laid ol' Shakespeare on them:

I did the same for the other subjects I'd asked them to describe. It worked perfectly—even the most reluctant scholars saw the majesty of expression in verse and the effectiveness of it.

Next class we read some more good poems, easy ones, and discussed why they were written and what they did. Then over the weekend I assigned them to write a one-page poem and said I wanted it good. No "roses are red, violets are blue" stuff. I got life-threatening glances and groans, but a conviction that they would end up with a bad mark if they didn't show up with a good poem. Most were convinced they couldn't, mainly because they'd never done it before. But they did, **every single one of them** in both of my senior literature classes. I had fifty-eight poems to take home and grade and what a pleasure it was. They were good, and some of the toughest cases in the school (pulling a strong "D" all the way through) really surprised me. Feelings are what make a poem, not grammar or spelling or necessarily structure. They had all moaned and made light of their masterpieces as they handed them in, but I detected a certain pride in them.

Good name in man and woman, dear my lord,
Is the immediate jewel of their souls:
Who steals my purse, steals trash; 'tis something,
nothing;
'Twas mine, 'tis his, and has been slave to
thousands;
But he that filches from me my good name
Robs me of that which not enriches him,
And makes me poor indeed.
                                        —Othello

The next day in class I told them we would read some more great poetry, and I began reading some of their works. None knew any different, except the individuals whose work I read and if you have ever seen self-esteem grow in a seat, it did with each kid when I read their verse and the others gasped in admiration, "Whose is that?"

My point was proven and they believed and many kept writing long after the classes ended. You see why I feel that anyone can write verse and love to do it. It is in every one of we humans. No one will ever convince me otherwise.

I know from observation, and from experience as a boss, parent, grandparent, and teacher, that verse has the power to persuade some greatness out of people when other motivations cannot. One of the students in my Lit class was a confirmed "D" student. Other teachers and the principal had fought his surly attitude for three and a half years and were preparing a party for his departure out of their school. He seemed in my class as they described him, "just sits there slumped over with a big sneer on his lips." Up to then, he was doing just the minimum necessary to maintain his "D" average. At the start of one class we entered into "Romanticism," and one of the things we discovered here was what a romantic presence the moon was in earlier days—the old poets and lovers had many fanciful imaginings of the moon. I challenged the class to do me a contrasting view of the moon, now that we had just landed on it. The students did the assignment in class.

I collected the papers and that night grading, I came across one that was a masterpiece. I read it to my wife (she was a four point student in college and quite the literary analyst). She said, "Wow, whose is that?" There was no name on it. The next day in class, I made a few comments about the poems they'd turned in and told them I would only read one and they would see why. When I read it out loud, the class gasped and wowed. I still didn't know whose poem it was. There were ten honor students among those present and a number of clever and accomplished writers. I read it again and told the class it was right up there with the masters and they agreed. The poem related love to the lunar cycles between moon and earth, and talked of affection in terms of atmospheric pressure and greater and lesser gravitational pulls. And it told its love story in terms of the very real geography and topography of the moon.

It was good (and I wish I had it for you).

"Who… whose?" everyone asked everyone else. I held it up and turned it around. "No name." I said. No one spoke up. "Come on now," I said, "it came out of here yesterday and you are all here. Whose is it?" The slumped over, sneering student finally raised one little pinkie acknowledging ownership. I walked back to him and laid the poem, with a large, red A+ on it, on his inactive arm and said, "Well Bob, you are out of my league and the rest of us, this is a masterpiece." He only grunted. The kid was brilliant, he never handed in a paper the rest of the year in my class under an A. He went on to write other good stuff, finished college, deflating and surprising every prediction in his behalf… and is doing well now. I'm convinced that poem was one of the triggers to completely change a life.

Poems have influenced and changed many. If not the reader, they **always** benefit the writer ...which could and even should be you.

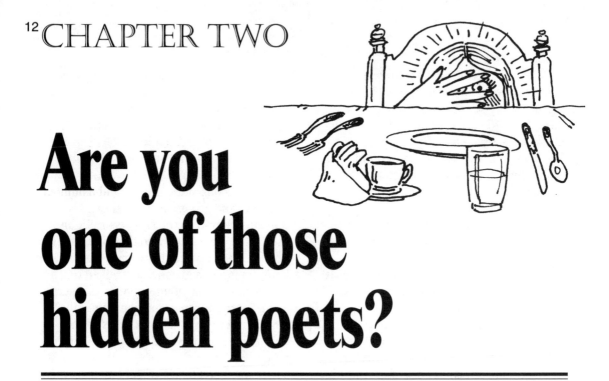

Are you one of those hidden poets?

My wife and I were at a family dinner once with many rather distant relatives— no one knew anyone too well. I was doing lots of TV at the time and my books were out there and some were bestsellers, so most of those present knew me. At a kind of awkward time and in an awkward way a father, positioning himself to get the full attention of me and others, removed a folded piece of paper from his pocket. "Mr. Aslett, I want you to hear this and tell me what you think." I heard a shriek of embarrassment from an attractive young mother across the room. It was one of her poems and she was fit to die. But the father, proud of his daughter, read the poem aloud, while she held her hand over her red face. But not entirely over—even in her total embarrassment, I saw one eye peeking out and asking, wondering, "do they like it?" It was good and I, the "master poet" in that residence said, "Wow, that is good, when did you write that?" People

clapped and asked her if she'd written any more.

I say good for her and good for that father and good for the poem. It made many of us happy that day, more than watching any of the multimillion dollar stuff on the TV would have.

I am constantly amazed by who can and will come up with poems. One night, well actually very early morning, in the cold Sawtooth Mountains of Idaho, I'd traveled nine hours from Arizona, across Utah. I was minutes away from snuggling in my warm bed at home, when a front tire blew on my car. Fixing a tire in zero weather isn't fun, but I'm fast and efficient and went for it, but no jack. My partner Arlo had borrowed it out of the company car. The lowest act in the world next to adultery, is to take someone's jack out of their car. I had to walk five miles through the forest, in below-zero temperatures, to get home. There was not a car in sight to stop and help me. I was going to call Arlo up and rail and rage and intimidate him, but that wasn't good enough, neither was beating. I thought for days how I could strike the hardest blow to repay him for the jack caper and you guessed it, a poem. I whipped out some verses, and this is how they started:

The Stolen Car Jack

That very night at 3 A.M., going
　　home so late,
The left front tire blew out, slowing
　　up my gait.
The spare was there, what a break,
　　as I opened the back,
But sad to see—
agony!—
no trace
of the
bumper
jack.

To my surprise, back in the mail just a few days later came a poetic response from my partner, describing the bad deal he got with his own company car. Arlo is a pharmacist and a violin player as well as a janitor. I had never seen him write a good job sheet or receipt yet, let alone a poem! But here is an excerpt from the long one he sent me:

The tires wear so quickly, 8000 miles or less,
The window doesn't work, man what a mess,
The hubcaps fall off so often they spin like a disk
The dogs never chase me—it's too big a risk.
It heats up so slowly you wouldn't believe
The length of the icicle that forms up my sleeve.

It is and always will be surprising, to see who among us writes poetry. It's sometimes the last person you'd suspect. Some poets will fess up, but others (including many with good verse) will never share their efforts or admit they love poems, to write them no less!

I hired a secretary for our publishing operation who was working toward a degree in media art, and had served an internship with ABC in New York. She and her husband, both in their early twenties, were struggling, as young married couples do, to get through school. They ran errands, sealed envelopes, helped with inventory—did all kinds of jobs. I gave her some of the poems in this book to type and help lay out. Several months later she said, "Back when I was young I wrote poems." I told her I'd love to read some. One day she timidly sneaked this onto my corporate mail pile—darn good, and she had even won a poetry prize with it!

Unison

While the hollyhocks sang
　　a vibrant song
　　and the sycamore
　　swayed in rhythm
You stood motionless
over the alabaster, looking
　　into a reflective glare
annoyed by the repetitive clinking
　　of droplets into the sink.
　　　　—Melissa Farrell

Come On... Admit It

I find it amusing, even pitiful sometimes, how many of the people who would like to put their

14

feelings in writing of some kind, never admit it. I'll often ask my audiences, "How many in here write their own poems, or would like to?" Only two or three hands may go up, when I know (I can even see some rough verse on their notepads), that probably half of them have written poems and most of the other half want to!

It's like singing—few of us do much singing, because we too often compare our efforts to Pavarotti or Streisand. We all like to sing and can, to one degree or another. And we will sing if and when we find a private place, such as to the kids or the cows or in the shower. But poems can be as private or public as you want them to be, from "for my eyes only" to being published on a billboard.

Most of us are romantics at heart. In the biggest, toughest redneck on a steel crew, the worn-down nurse in a nursing home, the bored deliveryperson or van driver, the wealthiest, and the poorest, awareness and sensitivity are always there somewhere. And really now, despite your job or busy schedule, you could find the time to express it. If you feel or see something that really moves you, stirs some old or new emotions, wouldn't it be nice to capture those feelings for yourself? Or even better... wouldn't you like to pass them on, be heard by others, at least a little? There aren't many avenues for personal expression anymore—TV, movies, radio, advertisements, tapes, cassettes, and computer programs of all kinds often absorb our feelings or distract us from them. So they often stay inside us. A verse, a poem, an essay, at least a line or two of the way we see and feel things is better than losing our insights and letting them pass.

What characterizes a "poet?"

About great feelings, great mysteries, I've always heard and read, "Only the poets know." Don't you believe it. Poets don't know or feel anything different from anyone else. They just happen to make the effort to write down what they feel and see.

All of us have the same basic senses of feel, smell, sight, hearing, taste, etc. We are limited only by how much we educate and exercise or fail to exercise these senses. People who like to write or read poetry are no smarter, better, more spiritual or intellectual than anyone else. They just seem a little more motivated to get to the bottom of life's "whys," to look a little more intensively at the course or sources of things, at hurts, highs, happinesses, and feelings in general. They seem to want to find answers to and sum up what's going on. In a way you might say that most poets are kind of quiet, polite rebels.

You'll never convince me that you cannot write verse, or that there is no purpose or place in your life for it. If a magic machine could extract the potential poetry within you, you'd be so taken aback you'd probably take a vacation just to catch up on reading and writing it. How much you write isn't the big issue either—

one good poem will do if it can have some profound effect on your life. You can go on to write scores or hundreds or thousands if it provides an avenue of self or public expression. Remember again the main value is to you, if you are the only one who likes your poems, that is colossal!

When my first few books came out, I hit the seminar circuit, doing workshops and classes for churches, clubs, school groups, and the like on the skills and fun of cleaning faster and better. At every seminar I handed out a "comment card" to collect some information from the attendees: the size of their family and house, how long it took them each week to clean, the jobs they liked and the ones they hated, the problem areas, and so on. The three hours of each seminar was a heavily filled block of time for the audience—listening and participating, and taking notes. You'd hardly expect people to find the time to fill out that card, but they did. And you wouldn't believe how many of the comments and observations came **in the form of a poem**: some two-liners, some longer. Here is just one sample:

There are a hundred ways to
    clean up dirt
And I know 81.
And so each day I clean and
    clean,
Isn't this such fun.
Now by the time I learn 6 more
And then know 87,
the dirt will still be all over
    here
And I'll be cleaning Heaven.
    —Jerry Witbeck

Poems like these sure get the drudgery of housework across, and give a big chuckle to those I read them to. Further evidence that ANYONE CAN WRITE POETRY!

Poetry is Fair Game for Anyone

No one owns poetry because they are famous or have had a lot published. We call some drivers "road hogs" because they take all of the road, but in verse, there are no takers or owners. Verse is there for the making and there is really no one out there (that counts) telling us what is good and what is bad. Maybe you don't like it, but if the author does, well... .

If it turns your crank to crank out poems, then even if no one reads them, they have great, great value. If they are read, even more value. If read, and liked, even published, then miracles will never cease for you!

> ### Just WHERE Does a Poem Come From?
> From an eight-year-old,
>   or maybe eighty,
> A lumberjack or
>   refined lady.

Poetry is not owned by anyone, there is no club or organization to get permission from—millionaires, intellectuals, English majors, or lovers. Poetry is fair game for everyone, educated or not. Even those who can't write can still rhyme for some goodness and quality of life. Even if those lines might only work once or twice and then be laid away or ignored, I still deem it a worthy investment. It **costs nothing** to produce and exercises some emotions or appreciation glands and muscles and Gadfrey, look what we pay professional seminar leaders or motivators who try to do that for us!

Poetry is not for the select few. You have as much of a right to write or read it as anyone on earth. That's quite a power when you think about it. Isn't the bottom line of poetry to make life more pleasant? Reading or listening to it is getting only one-half of its value. *Producing* some and actively using it in our life adds a dimension to life, and you don't have to be a pro at it, either.

In verse, there really are no amateurs. Who is poetry for, anyway? You first, others second. If you like it, it makes you feel good, fulfilled, then it's done a professional job. If others happen to like it too, then it's just an add-on to that already pro job. We really don't need to worry about social climbing via poetry, do we?

Nobody owns poetry any more than anyone owns conversation. You are just as much a poet in residence at your house or office as the most educated professor of literature and poetry, probably more so.

You are the master in your area of expertise—your own feelings, your friends and family, community, country, or state. Never hold back because you don't have any formal or fancy "credentials."

In sports sometimes there is a best boxer who owns the ring for a few years, a pitcher who owns the mound, a skater who owns the ice, but in writing **no** one owns the page at any age. Here there is a direct link to your brain, wit, desire, and ambition, and no middle man unless you mentally put one there.

If you publish a book of your poems and it only sells eight copies and you have to give the other one hundred and ninety-two or so you printed away (or save them for your grandchildren), even eight books that mean something to one other person besides you is a great accomplishment in my mind. It is worth it.

The biggest breakthrough in poetry you'll ever see, besides learning to love and use it, is when you find out you are or can be one with the masters. You'll never find out until you do it. Write what you feel and see and watch your face appear.

Emily Dickinson

John Greenleaf Whittier

James Whitcomb Riley

Edwin Markham

Walt Whitman

Sara Teasdale

YOU!

Ogden Nash

Henry Wadsworth Longfellow

Stephen Vincent Benét

Just for fun, here are fifteen quotes from "poets," seven from the masters and seven from your neighbors. Can you pick the seven masters? Try your luck. See what you think.

Masters vs Amateurs *Choose One* ✔

	A MASTER FROM THE PAST	A NOVICE LIKE US	Answer
I wrote some lines once on a time In wondrous merry mood, And thought, as usual, men would say They were exceeding good.	☐	☐	Oliver Wendell Holmes
They gave their all To the betterment of This nation founded On hope and love.	☐	☐	Robert L. Knox, janitor
I'm nobody! Who are you? And you nobody, too? Then there's a pair of us—don't tell! They'd banish us, you know.	☐	☐	Emily Dickinson
Or one, two, three, four Days of constant water roar A mesmerizing endless fount That tries to teach us not to count.	☐	☐	Grace Longeneker, homemaker
Fred the crab was a regular crab at least from what could be seen, his back was red and his front was white as many a crab's has been.	☐	☐	Trent Stephens, teacher
Six feet and over, Large-boned and ruddy, The eyes grey-hazel But bright with study.	☐	☐	Stephen Vincent Benét
The clouds, which rise with thunder, slake Our thirsty souls with rain; The blow most dreaded falls to break From off our limbs a chain.	☐	☐	John Greenleaf Whittier
Who through long days of labor, And nights devoid of ease, Still heard in his soul the music Of wonderful melodies.	☐	☐	Henry Longfellow
Why, who makes much of a miracle? As to me I know of nothing else but miracles, Whether I walk the streets of Manhattan, Or dart my sight over the roofs of houses toward the sky.	☐	☐	Walt Whitman
How pleasant was the journey down the old dusty lane, Whare the tracks of our bare feet was all printed so plane. You could tell by the dent of the heel and the sole They was lots o' fun on hand at the old swimmin'-hole.	☐	☐	James Whitcomb Riley

Remember… there are no amateurs when it comes to poetry. Poetry is the same as art, the big value is to yourself, not who buys it on the market. We don't do everything for money or value everything with the criteria of money… we don't do everything to make a living, we do most things **to enhance** living, or quality of life.

Poetry is for everyone, not just to read or listen to, but to write. It is time to move into another realm of poetry now, to start writing it. If you already are, then write more of it… it's wonderful, environmentally friendly therapy.

The great poets and great poems didn't end with the masters, great poems and great poets are being born daily, every minute, and you are, can be one of them, for yourself and others.

CHAPTER THREE

Why Poetry?

Why do we write Poetry?

Asking "why poetry" is kind of like asking why draw? Why decorate? Why sing? We can get along without any of these activities, but they enrich. Existence is something that just happens but "living" is the result of some enhancement.

If asked "why poetry" I wonder if any writer of it—any poet, master or beginner—could give an answer? Maybe "because I like to," simplistic as it sounds, might be the real answer. You'd probably get a pile of intellectual answers like "I write to change mankind" or "I write to express emotion" or "I write to vent anger or hostilities" or "I write to show off, get laughs," etc. I'd say the real bottom line is that poets write primarily for themselves.

Poetry should **enhance life**, and if only the author's, that's enough. Any more is pure bonus. After all what in life with all the food, cars, entertainment, sports, sex, we surround ourselves with, what are we trying to get anyway? Some joy and delight!

If the poem, the verse—yours or others—delights you, it has justified itself.

We write poetry for fun, self-satisfaction, to make others happy, maybe gain some popularity as life of the party or the family, maybe even to sell a verse or win a contest or two. There are probably twenty more hidden niches of good that come into a life from the use and writing of poetry, maybe even some off-the-wall things we'd never imagine.

I've met a number of people who write verse professionally for greeting cards and the like. And some have moved to writing lyrics for songs after their venture into poetry. There are many of you out there good enough to set up a little business at home, doing custom verses for people and their special occasions, just like an artist or magician would do. Even if you have to do some free at first to get known, and even if you only get a few bucks for some of your efforts, it all adds up to experience and building a base of satisfied clients. It's worth the effort if you love poetry and are good at it.

How Much Better Things Can Be Said in Verse

It truly is amazing how well, how much better something can be communicated in verse than even the most descriptive sentence.

For example: The grandfather is reading Jack in the Beanstalk and always notice when the giant speaks the grandfather's voice gruffs up, "FE FI FO FUM, I SMELL THE BLOOD OF AN ENGLISHMAN." The grandchildren quiver. What if that same message were given in ordinary words in a plain old statement? "Hey, there's a bloody bloke around here somewhere." No chills or hair standing on end there..

The rot and decay of things has long been written about and described—"depreciation" is what it's called in the business world. I've been to lectures and seminars on this subject and in all the volumes of words, written and spoken, nothing came close to this:

The Hammers

Noise of hammers once I heard
Many hammers, busy hammers,
Beating, shaping night and day,
Shaping, beating dust and clay
To a palace; saw it reared;
Saw the hammers laid away.

And I listened, and I heard
Hammers beating, night and day,
In the palace newly reared,
Beating it to dust and clay:
Other hammers, muffled hammers,
Silent hammers of decay.
            —Ralph Hodgson

Amazing how a single little verse can dramatize and clarify a thought. ... I heard this in school a hundred years ago and have used it myself for seemingly as many years:

It's the little things
that bother and put
us on the rack
You can sit upon a
mountain, but not
upon a tack.

Or what about the old favorite: "A stitch in time saves nine." Hark… it's dark… sure beats, "Boy, it sure is dark out here."

Why Poetry?

This girl had a sheep and it followed her.

A famous baseball player came up to the plate and failed to made a hit.

A blacksmith is at work underneath a big tree.

There are sermons, long lectures, books, even courses and classes that attempt to give us a message with profound meaning for our lives, just one little principle or precept we can remember and use. I've seen lots of single poems do the same thing in a few minutes. Here is one that accomplishes such work.

The Calf-Path

One day, through the primeval wood,
A calf walked home, as good calves should;
But made a trail all bent askew,
A crooked trail as all calves do.

Since then two hundred years have fled,
And, I infer, the calf is dead.
But still he left behind his trail,
And thereby hangs my moral tale.

The trail was taken up next day
By a lone dog that passed that way;
And then a wise bell-wether sheep
Pursued the trail o'er vale and steep,
And drew the flock behind him, too,
As good bell-wethers always do.

And from that day, o'er hill and glade,
Through those old woods a path was made;
And many men wound in and out,
And dodged, and turned, and bent about
And uttered words of righteous wrath
Because 'twas such a crooked path.
But still they followed—do not laugh—
The first migrations of that calf,
And through this winding wood-way
  stalked,
Because he wobbled when he walked.

This forest path became a lane,
That bent, and turned, and turned again.
This crooked lane became a road,

Where many a poor horse with his load
Toiled on beneath the burning sun,
And traveled some three miles in one.
And thus a century and a half
They trod the footsteps of that calf.

The years passed on in swiftness fleet,
The road became a village street;
And this, before men were aware,
A city's crowded thoroughfare;
And soon the central street was this
Of a renowned metropolis;
And men two centuries and a half
Trod in the footsteps of that calf.

Each day a hundred thousand rout
Followed the zigzag calf about;
And o'er his crooked journey went
The traffic of a continent.
A hundred thousand men were led
By one calf near three centuries dead.
They followed still his crooked way,
And lost one hundred years a day;
For thus such reverence is lent
To well-established precedent.

A moral lesson this might teach,
Were I ordained and called to preach;
For men are prone to go it blind
Along the calf-paths of the mind,
And work away from sun to sun
To do what other men have done.
They follow in the beaten track,
And out and in, and forth and back,
And still their devious course pursue,
To keep the path that others do.

But how the wise old wood-gods laugh,
Who saw the first primeval calf!
Ah! many things this tale might teach—
But I am not ordained to preach.
                              —Sam Walter Foss

How can a massive problem be summed any better than is done here:

Vice is a monster of so frightful mien.
To be feared needs but to be seen.
Yet oft familiar with her face,
We first endure, and then embrace.
—Alexander Pope

And how could you summarize the rules of social intercourse any better than this:

To live a life of joy and ease
Man mustn't say all he thinks
Or judge all he sees.

Just think of all the print and extended philosophy that could be eliminated by putting things in a verse or two. What a favor some poet has done for us all when they do this, the same favor YOU can do for yourself or others too!

Consider, too, all the efforts and measures in World War II to enhance security—meetings, memos, movies, lectures, posters, propaganda of all kinds. Some amateur poet came up with four words that had more impact than all the rest of the whole "security" movement:

"Loose lips sink ships!"

You're not convinced of the power of verse yet? Verse from the common person, I mean? Well, let's take it to the rock bottom—the toilet, the restroom stall. Now there, on the wall, is one of the largest and most enduring displays of literature found anywhere. Being a professional cleaner whose company cleans of millions of square feet of restroom every night, I deem myself a qualified judge. Sure there is smut and graffiti, which generally lives up to its reputation of offending and being forgot-

ten. But then there is the verse, those one or two or even four lines that someone painstakingly wrote on the wall, and almost everyone reads and remembers (admit it). You are a captivated observer, not to mention a captive audience. Of course you don't write or copy it down, you have more couth than that, but you can remember and repeat it better than the material just presented in the meeting! I don't like these stall scholars, but some of this verse shows talent!

Poetry Helps Us Remember Things

Poetry is a big help when it comes to memorizing and remembering things. We can collect data, absorb information, and hear sermons and lectures all our life, but great as it may be, calling it up when we need it is often impossible. We might have a faint recollection, but nothing like precise recall.

If something is said in rhyme or contains some alliteration (even a jingle), on the other hand, we will have it and keep it for years. Like the health summaries "Early to bed and early to rise..." and "An apple a day....," and those grade school memory aids "Thirty days hath September," "i before e, except after c," A B C D E F G, H I J K L M N O P.... and the like.

Likewise, I'll bet if you ask someone to quickly name a Revolutionary War hero, you know whose name would come first. Paul Revere! Why? We all know why— who could forget those first two lines that brought goosebumps and promise:

Listen my children and you shall hear
of the midnight ride of Paul Revere.

Who has ever forgotten "Humpty Dumpty"? A pretty silly little story when you think about it, but once we learn it as children, we remember it—forever!

We hear about something that happened, and no matter how big the event or how widely it is written about or announced, it gradually slips from our mind. But if someone says "Lizzie Borden"(a famous murderess of more than a century ago), you know immediately who that is, and even the details come immediately to mind. Why? A little verse someone did many years ago now:

> Lizzie Borden took an ax
> And gave her mother forty whacks.
> When she saw what she had done
> She gave her father forty-one.

Gruesome, yes, but engraved well in memory. Credit rhyme for this.

"I can't remember jokes." How many times have you heard or said that? I've probably heard thousands of jokes in my life, and if someone forced me to recall them right now ("tell or be shot!"), I couldn't remember many. I have a good memory, but the few I can recall all seem to have verse in them.

I remember one from high school, that was more than forty years ago now, about a father and mother's concern over their son's uncouth language. When they passed a sailor on the street, for instance, the kid would say "Hey, mom, look at that old bowlegged sailor." The parents decided to send the kid to Shakespeare school for some grooming and did. A year later he came home and they took him for a walk by the Navy base and again here came a sailor. The kid stopped, straightened his back, stood up tall, and sonorously said,

> What ho, what men are these
> that wear their legs in parentheses?

Not a much of a joke, but because of the rhyme, it and others I remember.

Why We Are Attracted to Poetry

We can and do have our strong likes and dislikes when it comes to food, art, scenery, vacations, and apparel, often completely opposite from each other, even if we are the same race, creed, color, family, sex, and line of work. Even music—it appeals to us all but we have some strong differences of preference here. But when it comes to poetry, for some magical reason it appeals to everyone, with far less of a spread of opinion.

Food is food, music is music, clothes are clothes, and words are words, but what makes plain old words arranged in rhythmic lines stand out? I believe it is inbred in us to be attracted to rhythm. It only takes seconds at a stadium to start up a chant—in no time at all everyone is stomping and clapping to the rhythm of the lines. Why does a train pull us into silent meditation, even in the midst of a noisy crowd? It is the consistent clickety-click, clickety-clack of the wheels on the track. The hoofbeats of a horse, likewise, get instant attention from us—nothing like a nice fast clippety-clop!

I remember back on the ranch how the belts and bearings of the combines and balers would have a rhythm and rhyme that almost demanded you write an imaginative poem to match it. I knew an astute Korean music teacher who gave voice lessons and also gave you something to think about for years. She said music's ability to win us over was so powerful because it didn't enter the brain to be processed, but instead was absorbed directly into our heart, and influenced our behavior almost without us realizing it. I believe this is true of poetry as well. People digest it and are nourished by it without having ever chewed or swallowed it. Amazing when you think about it!

People will respond to and obey music without a reason. Poetry is a close second here. The rhythm in words or music holds us. Perhaps that steadily beating heart of ours has an inborn feel for rhythmic beats!

Why Should You Write Poetry?

❒ For its value to you personally (whether anyone ever sees your poetry or not). The simple fact of disciplining yourself to the job of molding verses from your observations and feelings is a valuable training in expressing emotion in a lasting way.

❒ To express your opinion and ideas to others.

❒ To get attention, love, and respect, even from people who think you're a hard case.

❒ It's a wonderful way to preserve and remember something: a story, experience, bit of history, whatever.

❒ Poetry seems to have a therapeutic effect on us all. It can help settle things in your life, round up feelings and opinions and causes and injustices, and put them in a carryable case. Your poems (and those of others) can help give you better perspective.

❒ Another superb reason to write some of your own verse is that it will open other poetry to you, including some of those good master's verses. You'll be more sensitive to and appreciative of other verse.

BETTER THAN DOODLING!

I'm always intrigued, at home or on my travels, by how many people do crossword puzzles. Now these babies take brains, patience, study, sweat, even agony, and often some asking around. Too tough for me, for sure! Yet every trip I take, on planes, at airports, in restaurants, at any hour, on every side of me, are people pushing pencils toward a completed maze of the right words all in the right place. They labor hours on one of these puzzles and then **leave it behind** wherever they finished. I've never seen anyone ever keep this feat of wordsmithing, this evidence of accomplishment. Finished crossword puzzles aren't hung up or passed around or read to lovers and associates.

Granted this is a hobby and pastime, and it does give you some intellectual exercise. But taking that same energy of wordsmithing, careful word search and choice, and harnessing it into poetry instead would yield a much more satisfying and profitable product, reusable forever: your recorded emotions, what's in you, **up, down, and across!**

Poetry is for Sissies?

There is a "tough guys don't, tender guys do" stigma attached to poetry, an assumption that it is too delicate or sappy for real he-men or big businesswomen. According to this kind of thinking, poems are for children, Casper Milquetoasts, and sentimental, unaccomplished women— surely no big executive or hairy linebacker would invoke or involve themselves in verse! This is a laugh (we should write a poem about it, the fact that appreciation of poetry is the mark of a real red-blooded man or woman). The high and mighty—be they construction workers or world-renowned scientists—who don't or cannot gain insight and inner strength from the beauty and expressiveness of poetry, aren't the tough guys, they are wimps.

Too Early or Too Late to Start?

Poetry could be the first and last words you say, it has that capacity.

I know little kids of five, six, and seven years old that are coming up with rhymes and phrases that great, educated advertisers in downtown New York couldn't think of. I know we all think our grandkids are smarter than all the other millions of grandkids out there, but look at this one. Amanda, nine years old, wrote this after falling off a horse for the first time.

Bark, Buck... Tough Luck!

Let me tell you a story, about the day I rode a horse
It didn't have a happy ending, it had a happy start.
Oh Spud didn't want me on that horse so he bit the horse's toe,
And that's how it started, my friend, my exciting rodeo.
"Get out of here you, stupid dog," was a message Grandpa sent.
"Hang on, Hang on," yelled Uncle Stan as around and around we went!
The dog didn't stop, the horse didn't stop, what a fix I was in.
I was hanging on tight, with all my might, it didn't look like I could win.
Spud didn't want me on that horse, he was afraid I would get hurt,
And he wouldn't stop biting the horse until I hit the dirt.
Oh now you know the story, about the day I rode a horse,
It didn't have a happy ending, it had a happy start!
—Amanda Clark, 1993

There was an elderly woman who wrote and wrote poetry for our local newspaper. The older she got, the more poems came out and why not—her verses only got better with time. Age has a deep mine of experience (and greater marketing capacity—just think of all the relatives to read your poems to!).

Age, location, education, vocation, make no difference when it comes to prowess in poetry.

What's going on here in this cross-section of everyday people? (you are in here somewhere). All of them like some kind of poetry and have been influenced profoundly by it some time, maybe everyone in the picture, and maybe that influence is still strong. And most of them want to write their own poem or two, and all of them can. But the truth of the matter is, few of them do. So lots of people are missing some real satisfaction and accomplishment needlessly, and why?

Not lack of talent, not lack of feeling, not lack of ideas or subject, just a simple lack of starting. This is a good time in life to start.

What Are You Waiting For?

We have lots of things labeled "bad" these days...and one of them is waste. We are usually thinking in environmental terms here and often do not carry the "evil" of waste over to our own time and talent. I think it is just plain pitiful to see waste in human resources, or in other words the emotion, energy, and talent of you and me. And we do waste, don't we? Through neglect, laziness, lack of confidence, or because we're "short of time."

I often wonder why we don't do the things we really want to and the things we can. All around we see it...singers who don't sing, craftspeople who don't craft, artists who don't sketch, teachers who don't teach, comforters who aren't comforting, fathers who don't do fatherhood, statesmen who aren't stating...and... (I know they are out there) millions of poets who aren't composing.

Do you wonder what we are all waiting for? When will we start? Think of all the love and life and days we are missing right now.

Just think of all the times you've read a poem that said something you have seen and felt and wanted to say—and it said it so perfectly you will always remember it. Wouldn't it be wonderful to do this for yourself with your own verse, and maybe even have others find in you what you have found in other poets? It would be one of one of those true high points in life.

Let's Put Poetry Back in Its Place!

There is a tendency in all of us, even the youngest, to sigh over the "good old days" as compared to "the world today." Poetry had a big part in my own "good old days"— it was read at get-togethers, in the evening with the family, when courting, even over the radio.

While putting this book together, I checked out not just the family bookshelves but the local libraries to round up all the poem books I could and surprisingly found only a few. All the rest were either worn out, lost, or had been loaned out or given away. I had my all-time favorite poems in my notebooks and speaking ledgers, but the hundreds of others I loved were just not around.

A few weeks later I was scheduled to do a full Saturday of autographing in three of the West's largest bookstores, so I figured I'd get a new supply of "poem books." I arrived at the stores two hours early to set up my table and look around, see what was there. All three of them are truly major book dealers, and I walked every aisle and failed to find a poetry section. I found a few nursery rhyme collections for kids, but adult poetry was nowhere to be found. Finally I got the manager of one of these places and he led me to a corner in the farthest end of the store. There were thirty two-sided islands in that store, each with fourteen compartments of books, which added up to 420 compartments in all. What was in them? They were loaded with books about crime, sex, and murder (which had two dozen sections), self-help and recovery had fourteen, business had seventeen sections, diets and food had around thirty, and horror/mystery about twenty racks. Poetry in its entirety had one and a half sections. Dogs and cats even had more than all of poetry!

I guess that is reality and what people today like. I say they are missing out and if twenty racks were filled with good poetry (including poems authored by good people like you), the crime, self-help, and recovery book islands would shrink all by themselves to make room for them.

Poetry is one of the few life expanders like faith, hope, and charity.

CHAPTER FOUR

Getting Started

What Can We Write About?

Some people never get started because they "can't think of anything to write about." That is an incredibly feeble excuse for just about any of us—it's just plain old failure to pay attention to what's going on around you. Daily we probably run into at least a dozen topics that could be effectively cast in verse. The great poet Robert Burns wrote a poem to a mouse—a pretty clever one, too. If a mouse merits a poem, then so do cockroaches, geckoes, clothespins, campfires, flat tires, aerosol containers, and road graders. Longfellow wrote a verse to a skylark and a cuckoo and even some daffodils, Robert Frost to a hired man, Carl Sandburg wrote about grass, Elizabeth Bishop about fish, and Richard Wilbur

about a potato. We people in modern days are exposed to at least a hundred times the objects, people, and events that any of these earlier poets were. You probably have **five hundred times** the topics to choose from than they had, so go ahead, do it—pick a point, a position, a pet, a picture in the mind and poem it!

Remember the times in the normal course of a day when you or someone else suddenly broke into a grin or were amazed by something? Or during a dull, drawn-out meeting suddenly began chuckling to yourself? We've all had a flood of perception, anger, passion, power, or greed sweep through us, or felt total disgust at having been left out or picked on. A poem can and will capture anything efficiently before it passes away forever.

When and why write a poem?

- [ ] A mood
- [ ] An injustice
- [ ] A humorous event
- [ ] A cause
- [ ] A feeling
- [ ] A failure
- [ ] The weather
- [ ] The seasons
- [ ] Congratulations
- [ ] A story
- [ ] A person
- [ ] An animal
- [ ] A dream
- [ ] A game
- [ ] A trip
- [ ] A date
- [ ] A job
- [ ] A joy
- [ ] A disappointment
- [ ] A fear
- [ ] A hope
- [ ] Any news
- [ ] A friend
- [ ] A lover
- [ ] A vision
- [ ] A thought
- [ ] A gain
- [ ] A loss
- [ ] An illness
- [ ] A memory

These and hundreds more things are happening around and to you daily. Some are too good or too bad to let slip away. Grab them! Share them! Relive and remember. That's what poetry can do.

Finding Poems

Poems can pop out of the strangest places
Sum up ideas and make magic faces
From a text, a map, memo, or list,
A verse can keep meaning from being
   missed.

You may be asking, Now just when and where do you FIND a poem? The sources are endless and free, too. When you come across something memorable in a newspaper, letter, ad, conversation, or elsewhere, create some lines out of it.

One man, for instance, telling me about his mounds and piles of junk and clutter (which he'd finally had his fill of), suddenly blurted out: "Sentiment can become sediment!" That had a ring to it, so I jotted down:

> Sentiment kept in pile or print
> Left unstirred becomes sediment.

Another time, a hardworking hospital administrator came up with a classic statement one day as he discussed with me the many years he'd spent setting up the groundwork for his business. I jotted it into poetry, calling it Bernie's Beatitude:

Bernie's Beatitude
The Lord knows I can be
humble when I'm poor
Cause I've struggled for every stitch,
But I'd like to show him
through opportunity
I can also be humble
when I'm rich.
—Bernie Box, 1979

The key here is when something (seen, heard, or felt) strikes a chord. Whether it's one word, one line, or a description of a witty circumstance, jot it down. You don't need to convert it into a verse right then, just capture and record it. Our first instinct, first appraisal usually proves to be best. You can always expand on and enrich it later, but trying to recall it later with nothing to help you out can be pure agony.

Does Everything We Write Have to Be 100% Original?

We like to think everything we write or say is original, but how much we pick up from others and incorporate into our writing would probably shock us all.

There's nothing wrong with redoing a theme or subject that's already been done, or doing another angle on something that's already been done—you have the right to do this. As long as you're not actually *copying* anything, just be honest and sincere as you can and rhyme away.

Smaller Targets May Be Better at the Start

Many people don't write the verse they could because they are trying for too wide an audience, trying to cut too wide a swathe—in other words making their poem too broad for any use.

At first we often write poems that are very general, hoping for an audience of everyone. We soon discover that all poems don't fit everyone, some of our best will be done for just one or two or a few people, an occasion, a shared experience, a surprise, a hello, a good-bye, a coming or a leaving, a getting or a giving—a specific, not a general, all-world occasion.

Verse that is too wide in scope, reforming the world or an entire nation and everyone in it, is a lot tougher than sticking to a local or regional, or better still, a very personal and individual message.

Don't Always Write the Same Kind of Thing

Venture a little out of your "favorites" or old standbys and learn to write in different categories: for the family, for work, romance, animals, nature, sports, food, and so on. The more categories you have, the more easily you can pick what fits you and the occasion. Be flexible, people who only write about the wind or the rain or the sunset will end up with rather weather-beaten, dull stuff eventually.

Take the Time to Find the Best Angle on the Subject

I knew a guy who seemed to always have the best pictures I'd ever seen. He did have a nice camera, but so did I, and his pictures were… just better, clearer, more dramatic, better composed, etc. He chuckled when I expressed my disappointment about my own pictures compared to his. "Ho! You take as good or better pictures than I do," he said. "You just don't take as many and sort them down to the best." He said the most valuable thing he'd learned going to photography school was that film is the cheapest part of taking pictures. Where we generally take one or maybe two of the subject, they taught him to take five or six or even ten, and out of the bunch one or two were always superior.

Likewise, pen and paper are the cheapest part of writing good verse. When you see a subject, write not one view or two but maybe a quick eight or ten angles on your idea and then pare them down to the one that really works.

Poetry Doesn't Have to Be Heavy to Be Good

Every time I get around the intellectual crowds and hear the big name poets and quotes from them tossed around like a rhythmic football, I always stop and wonder: if we really took count right now, among all people in the US or the world (and didn't include poems that were school assignments, which most of us wouldn't have otherwise read) if poets like Ogden Nash, Richard Armour, Edgar Guest, Dorothy Parker, Robert Service, and Rod McKuen are not read, re-read, and enjoyed more than most of the "masters."

When I timidly introduced some of my first writings, I figured there must be a multitude of pros out there to learn from. So when I saw an ad for a writers' conference at a local university I signed up. There was a multitude there all right, all just like you and me, common folk with the desire to maybe write something to feel good about. There were a few who thought they were pros but I saw and heard nothing exceptional from them.

That evening they had a special feature—the "poet in residence" from one of the big faraway universities who was to read his poems. We all went, and he read...

"The dew dropped on the heads of wheat so it hung downy"

or something like that. As he read on, there were a few polite pitter pats of clapping from the metal-framed glasses section, but ninety percent of us looked at each other with an "Am I missing something?" look. The guy was chloroform on the hoof, his material chloroform on the page. Many of us left really inspired that night—if this person rated "poet in residence" at a major university, then our poems had a real future!

For years I've subscribed to the writers' magazines and read the columns of the poets and I've clipped and saved a fair amount of their stuff. Its difference is recognizable alongside of all the amateur poems sent to me by fifth graders and up. Much "pro" writing is so heavy, you can't understand what it is saying without re-reading, stopping to think, looking up a word or two, and asking the teacher. Maybe I'm a little dumb, but it often is beyond me.

One morning my wife and I were taking a bus from the foot of the mountains at Juneau, Alaska, to the coast to catch a ship on to Skagway. The bus driver, an elderly man with senior citizen silk-white hair, picked up the loudspeaker mike and pointed out the glaciers and the creeks for a few miles as he drove. Then he asked if he could embark on a recitation of one of his favorite Alaskan poems. The passengers clapped, "Yes!" The man was silent for a minute as the bus slipped through a tunnel of moss-covered oceanside trees. Then as he rolled into the first two lines, my heart went to my throat... Robert Service! Man, could that guy write poetry, and man, could that bus driver recite it. He had the bus spellbound telling of the Eskimo giving his life to save his wife in a boat wreck. I thought I owned all of Robert Service's works, but I hadn't heard this one and I was leaning so far over the seat bar of the bus, my arm and leg went numb. We all had to take a big sigh to get our breath when he ended. For the rest of the way, I chatted with the driver about why Robert Service was so great and that driver taught me a lot about poetry.

In Robert Service's poetry, you know exactly what he said and what he meant and what the people in the poems felt. Right at that instant. You don't have to pause or puzzle or backtrack or look up words or rethink. You just live it as it happens! I feel this is a secret of good poetry. What could be better than creating understanding and feeling? That is about it. Who does that the best or well, is the best and a good poet. Nothing else really counts in verse or writing, does it?

Look at these lines from Mr. Service, for example:

If that verse doesn't fit the corporate scene—gold and power and the result of it—nothing does. Service took the mining field and business and education and all fields of life and put them right in that verse.

"The Shooting of Dan McGrew" and "The Cremation of Sam McGee" are the most popular and often quoted poems of Service's. But his masterpieces are the others. Buy his collected verse and curl up in a down comforter and turn the furnace up to 89 and watch your self shiver as you read… and feel the power of poetry!

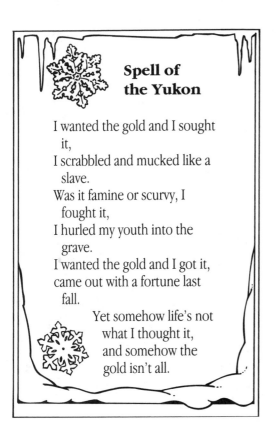

Spell of the Yukon

I wanted the gold and I sought it,
I scrabbled and mucked like a slave.
Was it famine or scurvy, I fought it,
I hurled my youth into the grave.
I wanted the gold and I got it,
came out with a fortune last fall.
Yet somehow life's not what I thought it,
and somehow the gold isn't all.

What Poems Do People Read and Enjoy Most?

The ultimate test of poetry isn't whether critics and scholars say it is good, educational, or acceptable, but the effect it has on readers.

What poems do people read and enjoy most? If there was a count of how many times things were read for sheer enjoyment (not because they were assigned in class), I wouldn't be surprised to see Richard Amour way ahead of Samuel Coleridge.

Personally I would not attempt to define "proper poetry." The only thing that determines worth is result: value or significance—not only to readers, but to the writer. If a modest little "moon in June" line or two is precious writing or great reading for you, then again I say it is "good stuff."

Stop Worrying about All the Rules and Definitions

Don't get hung up on all the "structural laws" of poetry or verse. There are and always will be in every area of life, people who sit around and make up definitions, boundaries, and directives for the activity in question (they seldom actually practice the activity or enjoy it). Forget the protocol of poetry—what works for you has worth. I know that when I'm tackling a personal assembly project or assignment, if there are over three directions I generally drop it and move on to something else. Many of us are like this, so getting bogged down in "proper procedure" is sure to discourage us, perhaps permanently!

Remember, there are no set ways to write poetry. You might invent a better way that even the seasoned scribes have never thought of, so don't be obsessed or intimidated by the idea of "properness." First go for the end result of expressing your feelings or getting your message across in a concise, interesting, and somewhat rhythmic fashion. Then work from there— **rough it and then right it!**

Don't hold back because you don't know proper English

Don't procrastinate because you don't know how to punctuate. You wouldn't think of not making a snowman because you don't know precisely where to put the eyes or the arms. I see some expert grammarologists argue for thirty pages in a book as to the exact place a semicolon or comma might go to be used properly. For now just make up your own rules and get on with it. Who knows and who really cares?

The Boundaries of Beneficial Verse

There are some boundaries for ending up with a beneficial verse, however. One big one is that there needs to be some **cause, purpose, or direction** in a poem. Whether you are writing about the wreck of the *Titanic*, or a date that ended up a proposal, writing about a loss or a victory, a refusal or a request, there must be a message—the poem needs to be going somewhere and for some reason.

A poem needs to have a purpose— rainbows, sunrises, or frost crystals, matter how beautiful or mystical, won't quite do it all by themselves. Pretty leaves falling off trees and birds fluttering their wings on a high branch or hail thundering on a roof on a lonesome day, etc., are great to write about. But take them in a direction. You can write some waste getting there (stuff you don't end up actually using), don't sweat it. But whether you're just doing some verse for fun, or because you feel like commenting on something, it will help to make sure those lines take you and others somewhere. Poems about a bell tinkling in the breeze, water dripping from the eaves, or frost shining on the sheaves are too likely to leave the reader thinking, "so what?"

Poetry should be productive—it should tickle, probe, motivate, dry a tear, even bring a tear. You don't have to have a life and death reason for the existence of a verse, but you do need a direction or a reason. Keeping this in mind helps make sure you write something others will want to read.

HOW DO I DO IT NOW?

Where do I start? There are thousands and thousands of "how to" books and seminars a year, on every subject imaginable. Going through bookstores, and my high school and college texts and books of literature, however, I haven't found much on the basic mechanics of how to write poetry. And what I have found is often pretty technical.

My opinion, before you search the shelves for the last word in "how to," is that you should just launch out on your own. Do some poems and verses formatted like others you've liked. "Want to" will accomplish 95% more than "how to." I've noticed that many people who enthusiastically absorb and bury themselves in how-to books never seem to get to the **do**-do of the activity in question. It's kind of like being so busy consulting the schedule that you miss the train.

In this book you will find a short "mechanics of verse" from a common person's viewpoint. My approach isn't academic, but it is simple and quick.

The Tools

Personally, I haven't used a pencil and eraser for twenty-five years. I'm a pen person. I love the dark, easy to read, promise-not-to-go-away result of a pen. I don't like to erase things and rewrite them. If I make a mistake on my roughs, I just cross it out and write above it. Ink has a commitment that pencil lead lacks!

Again here, heart, mind, and hand are about 98% of what you need to tackle a poem. Most good verse won't come to you when you're in front of a typewriter or computer, or have dictaphone in hand. It will strike when you're in the front seat of a grain truck or the back seat of a crowded bus, in the shower, lying ill in a hospital bed, or still quivering from an emotional beating. This will usually be poem time and grabbing whatever is at hand—a board, a napkin, or a Crayola is good enough. Save the mechanical wizardry and fancy typefaces and printers for revising and perfecting your poems. Don't be like the person who "can't run today because my headset is broken."

The Three Most Important Ingredients of a Poem

Once you have a good idea for a poem, there are three important ingredients for a poem after that:

RHYMING, TIMING, AND CLIMBING

Rhyming: Whether words are written or heard, they always seem sweeter when they rhyme.

Timing: Make the poem fit the event, feeling, or emotion, like a ski poem fits in winter.

Climbing: As I said earlier, a poem has to have a message or meaning, has to go somewhere, to have a purpose. (That purpose could be to change or criticize something, entertain the reader, or get their sympathy for something). It has to answer "Why does this poem exist?"

As far as the rest of it—the mechanics of structure, style, size, grammar, and the

34

like…. Folks, in poems as long as it works, you can get away with anything!

Using a Ready-Made Structure

Lots of we first-time poets use a familiar, easy poem as a structure to put our message in, like "The Night Before Christmas." I've seen takeoffs on that in dozens of tailor-made verses:

Twas the night before trash day and all through my closet, I knew in the dumpster, I should make a deposit.

Longfellow and "The Village Blacksmith" have launched many a beginning poet, too.

Under the spreading coconut tree,
A lowly beach bum stands
Unemployed by heck, with a welfare check
in his large and greedy hands.

My six-year-old granddaughter came up with:

Twinkle, twinkle, Little star,
If you smoke, you won't go far.

You don't have to stick with the masters, or Mother Goose's outline forever, but borrowing a framework to use as an initial mold or pattern is a good way to get started.

Jotting Down the Elements and Then Putting Them Together

Let's go through a sample of writing poems this way.

We've all camped out, most of us have slept in a tent or a sleeping bag, up in the mountains or out on the plains somewhere. Let's say this is an experience you want to capture or share. So mentally you make a list of your impressions and recollections here, then write them down:

always a rock or root to gouge me— the bag slips downhill—it's too cold, or too warm—pine needles/spiders in bag, mosquitoes outside—no pillow—the zipper gets stuck when I try to get in or out—bag gets wet—wake up stiff, etc.

Now just pick and choose and tell your story. It helps sometimes here to arrange the ideas or images in their logical or natural order of appearance or happening.

Sleeping Bag in the Mountains

I pick a spot to spread my bag
To view the midnight sky
But every time there is a rut
Or rock beneath hip or thigh.
And should it slant one half degree or more
That ground where I camping lay
Sunrise will find the bag and me
Over twenty feet away.
Leaves get in, I can't get out
Of that bag of torture design
I crick my neck and freeze my snout
It happens every time.

Now type it up and pass it around to all your camping buddies, they will get a charge out of it—a poet's mission accomplished.

P.U,N;C:T!U"A'T-I?O]N.

I know there are rules and proper ways to do things when it comes to punctuation, and that those little marks can greatly influence the effect of a word or line. But even though I've taught high-school English, I'm a free thinking, anything goes punctuator when it comes to **any** writing. I use quotation marks, parentheses, exclamation points, dashes, and slashes all over the place. (My editor and other grammarians take many of them out in my published work, so as not to offend the intellectuals.)

The important thing to remember here is that poems do have a sentence structure and periods, commas (and capitalization) should be used when needed to start, stop, and break a line, just like we learned back in sixth grade. Overdoing the exclamation points, dashes, commas, and the like effects like is OK and even good in a first draft, it helps accent the point. When you go back over the poem to brush it up you can tone them down a little.

The same is true of "typographical special effects" like boldface and underlining, oversize or undersize type. A little of this sort of thing is good and can help highlight and bring home your message. Just don't overdo it—not even the biggest, blackest, boldest type will affect the reader as much as a well chosen word.

Art Thou Thinking of Using Special Language?

Most of we modern folks aren't too familiar with or even comfortable using the "poetic" or "biblical" type of wording that often appeared in poems of the past, which we could call "Hallowed Language." You know the kind I mean: words like 'tis, 'twas, thou, thee, thine, doth, hath, yea, etc. If you feel it somehow makes a poem more "official" to use them, go ahead, no one owns them and few these days know anymore about them than you do.

If you want to make a poem sound old or "traditional," or sometimes even for comic effects, language like this does in handy.

In general, take it easy with special language, dialects, and the like in verse. Be sure your intended audience will understand any unusual terms you intend to use, and remember that attempts to reproduce regional dialects, foreign accents, and the like in writing can get tiresome if not incomprehensible.

Titling Poems

It's your poem! Call it what you want but don't be one of those indecisive perfectionists who sits down to an empty page, can't come up with a great title, so they never start the poem. Tap a temporary title on a poem at first if necessary, so you won't lose or confuse it. Then as you work your way through it pick out the word or thought that best expresses or describes who or what the poem is about and use it. If nothing comes to you, use the first line of the poem as a temporary title. When you're in mid-poem, or just as you're finishing it, the title will come.

If you're really baffled, ask someone else to read it and suggest, or call it "Ode to _____[the subject]". Days, weeks, or years later a better title may come along. So change it!

A title can be like dousing a poem with chloroform or starter fluid, one puts to sleep, the other sparks! A little explanation, or touch of drama in a title always helps: "Casey at the Bat" is better than "Casey," "The Cremation of Sam McGee" is better than "Cremation," "Wreck of the Hesperus" better than "Hesperus." A flowery title is OK for some kinds of verse; long titles seldom get read; one-word titles are great but risky.

Naming a poem is part of the fun!

WHEN Should You Write Poems? STRIKE WHILE THE EMOTION IS HOT!

When you write, in my opinion, is more important than how you write or even what you write about. We all rely on feeling, mood, and motivation to spark the flame. We don't all have the same habits or the same pattern to our daily ups and downs, but we all have more commitment, power, energy, and yes, nerve at certain times than others. I know there is a power time to tap in us and when it comes, when feeling good or bad is flooding your being, grab a pencil. Or if your computer's handy, run to it and roll! Capture the thought while it is there in your heart or in your head. If you wait until it's convenient, generally you lose the edge, the impulse, the spirit of the cause you were invited to express (and often some of the information you need).

Once after several eighteen-hour, no rest, skipped meals, rush-rush days in a row, I came to the conclusion I was tired. I'd tried several times to describe it, but always the next morning or afternoon when I was rested and caught up with things. Then I took a trip to St. Louis in which I

did presentation after presentation with crowds and stress and pressure. It was into bed at 1:00 A.M., up early, and then eight straight hours in hotel meeting rooms doing teaching that required the highest energy level. I was so tired, I was staggering like a drunkard. When I finished up at last I dashed to the airport with tons of baggage and a giant trunk. The plane ride back took forever, and it would land far from my home in the middle of night. Then I would have to drive (half unconscious) 250 miles home. Sitting in my plane seat too tired to even eat, I felt and knew tired like never before. Now was the time to capture it, so I wrote my summary of it.

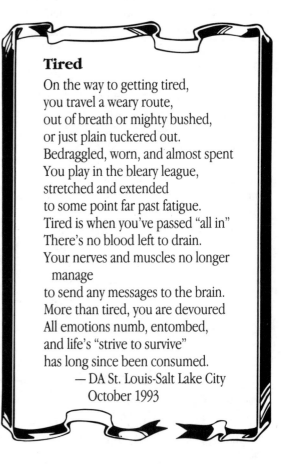

Tired

On the way to getting tired,
you travel a weary route,
out of breath or mighty bushed,
or just plain tuckered out.
Bedraggled, worn, and almost spent
You play in the bleary league,
stretched and extended
to some point far past fatigue.
Tired is when you've passed "all in"
There's no blood left to drain.
Your nerves and muscles no longer manage
to send any messages to the brain.
More than tired, you are devoured
All emotions numb, entombed,
and life's "strive to survive"
has long since been consumed.
— DA St. Louis-Salt Lake City
October 1993

If you have just been fired, jilted, blessed with a new child, hit by a tornado, shipwrecked, bankrupted, passed over, insulted, well fed, or not fed at all, now is the time to go for it. If you wait until later and try to remember it and write it down, you'll lose the edge, the crisp, full spirit of the feeling. When to write it is NOW, when the feeling is ripe or the wound is still raw, when passions and ideas are pouring through you—not later when you are in a neutral mood trying to catch up on things! So do it now, and even if you have to miss the movie or the meal.

Poems with an edge are generally better done when you are on the edge. You need to tap into that turmoil while it is there, don't wait until the music, headache, event, trauma, or disaster is over and you are home and dry and restored and safe and mellow. Write it when you are wet and cold, hot and thirsty, discouraged or despairing. Even angry is okay (but when you write in anger be sure to wait and reread and perhaps revise before sharing the poem with anyone).

> When you see, hear, feel, see, taste, or sense something, jot it down, even a word or line or sentence, and store it as firewood for your poems' fire.

Finish it now, too

I'm pretty disciplined, but I've noticed that poems or essays that I start in great gusto and then lay aside until later, I often never finish. I go back and peck and plod at them, but my mortar for the structure is hard and it won't go together. If you cannot build it now when you're feeling it most, you may find it much harder to pick it up and flesh it out and finish it later.

You can (and should) always go back and fine-tune your rhymes to perfection and maybe replace a word or two, that makes a better verse. But get the whole of the message—the structure and outline and basic rhyme—done in one sitting if you can. Changing a line or two is refinement and is fine to do later, but get it framed from the first and the message clear. Do it now—all at once, don't even go to the bathroom or to get a drink of juice when your juices are flowing…finish…finish!

> **Write it now!** Don't wait for the perfect mood and time to write what you feel, step aside at the party or sit down beside the trail and write it now!

I remember once when one of the key members of my maintenance crew finked out—he didn't put forth an effort, he took the easy way out and let the project fail. Because it was "hard" (as he put it). I ripped out a pad in the pickup and wrote like crazy. The result was a little rough but it told the tale.

The Easy Way

It's easier to see a hero than to be a hero.
It's easier to wish it out than to dish it out.
It's easier to join a group than to organize one.
It's easier to eat the game than hunt it.
It's easier to die than it is to live.
Virtue takes more effort than vice
So pity the person who likes everything nice.
You'll dissolve in life like sugar in water
If you never learn that sometimes, well, life isn't what it "oughter"!

Another time I was just walking along when my mind was suddenly on the side of a fishing stream with my dad. He was the most expert manager and efficient doer I ever knew, and the best fly fisherman. With him you kept and lived by the rules. And you learned the true meaning of responsibility. Thinking of all this, I immediately jotted this, one of my better efforts, down.

Remember the best and deepest feelings or experiences don't come when you are in the mood or ready to write them down. Don't lose them, however—especially if they have elements that apply to everyone, get them down. If it caused you to "wow" at the time, the experience is generally well worth recording and even sharing with others.

When Do You Write Poems? All The Time! Anytime, Anyplace, on Anything, with Anything!

The Rule of Responsiblity

My father always taught to me... the Rule
  of Basic Responsibility.
At fishing when I caught a batch, he said,
  "Son, you always clean your catch."
One day my luck ran zero slim—all the fish
  bit just for him.
He dumped his trout at my feet, saying
  "Son, some help would be so neat."
I quoted back his ruling fair: what he
  caught, he must prepare!
He said, "Son, the second rule is hard to
  beat, for my catch is all you get to eat."
So I cleaned his catch thankfully, for
  another basic responsibility.

CHAPTER FIVE

Time to rhyme!

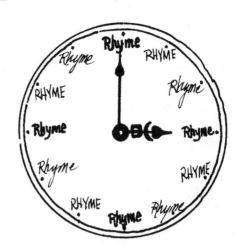

Much of the pleasure of poemcrafting comes from making our lines "echo" each other—even the most ordinary thoughts are more fun, memorable, and interesting in rhyme. You might call rhyming the process of making the notes you are taking on the world anyway a little nicer.

Working with Rhyme

Any poem starts with an idea—a thought, experience, event, or feeling— that rings a bell, strikes an emotional chord in you. Jot it down, capture it, in a few words, a sentence, or a paragraph. Something everyone laughed or clapped for, or loves to hear about, is generally something you and others will enjoy seeing recorded.

Like...

- The time Grandma drove home without her glasses
- The time that "placid old" saddle horse bolted and ran!
- Got snowed in for three days
- Your adventure trip or special visit
- Your old faithful car (which you love dearly) finally died
- First time blueberry picking in Alaska!
- The shock we're never prepared for— the kids' room

Let's put down a line or two and work with it now, using the "dirty kid's room" idea as an example.

I opened the door, what a disastrous shock!

Now what would rhyme with shock?
mock   smock   knock   lock
SOCK   SPOCK   talk   hawk
ROCK   stalk

Of this list three could fit, so let's fit them in now:

I opened the door, what a disastrous shock!
To be slapped in the face with a filthy sock
There was a piece of ear from Dr. Spock
And the jam on the knob was as hard as a rock.

The next line could describe what the room smelled like:

The odor that issued from under the bed

OK, now what rhymes with bed:
said   fed   DEAD   DREAD   head
sped   red   NED   med   lead
So we might go to this now:

The odor that issued from under the bed,
it had to be something totally dead.
To even look under, filled me with dread,
(I finally located deceased Uncle Ned).

Don't be afraid to write four, five, or even a half dozen lines that might fit in a given spot, till you find one you really like. Then as your poem comes together you can go back and recycle some of the others to fit into the rest of the poem.

Now here's an important little "poet's secret." Let's say the next line is:

There were weenies and Wheaties stuck to the covers.

Now we look for a rhyme to "covers."
Lovers   shovers   hovers
abovers   glovers

There isn't anything that fits or makes sense. When this happens, too many poets try to force one of the available rhyming words to fit and end up with a weak or awkward rhyme. For some reason very few will look up and change the initial line. Let's do that now, and change "cover" to "blanket."

Almost zero that goes with that:
blanket   sank it   rank it
So let's change it to…

There were wieners and Wheaties stuck to the quilt.

Now:
built   jilt   HILT   SILT   tilt
SPLIT   wilt   guilt   stilt
Bingo—lots of choices here!

There were weenies and Wheaties stuck to the quilt
A corner with pizza crusts filled to the hilt
Fallout from footwear, two foot of silt
Stains on the pillow where root beer was spilt.

As you get into the poem stop and visualize the room, the event, the feeling, and quickly write it down. Don't worry about order or organizing now. When the ten or so random verses are done you can shuffle and adjust them to come up with a suitable verse.

The sheer enjoyment of it all, writing verse—sitting there all alone, no other input, just you and a pencil and one piece of paper, or a keyboard and blank screen. Then after some frowning and brow-wrinkling, you hit the right word or rhyme and start saying to yourself, "That's not bad....in fact, it is goooooood!" (This is not really conceited, just excited.) You start grinning and chuckling to yourself as you see things coming together and start structuring some verse. Onlookers might deem you weird, but so what!

Rhyme Patterns

Your "rhyme pattern" can be all lines rhyme, every other line rhymes, every third line rhymes, internal rhyme within the lines, etc. For example, in the poem we've been discussing, rhymes within every other line might work:

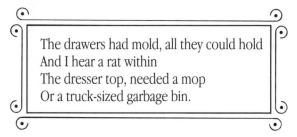

The drawers had mold, all they could hold
And I hear a rat within
The dresser top, needed a mop
Or a truck-sized garbage bin.

Here is another type of rhyme pattern that could be used:

I held my breath
To avoid sudden death
This room would surely get me,
The dog wouldn't stay
In that room anyway
I don't think he'd even leave pet pee!

What a variety of types of verse there is—some poems have distinct rhyme patterns, others are little different than plain prose. Take it from there and do your thing!

All of the following types of internal rhyme (rhymes within a line itself), work, for example.
- 1 word: HeeHee
- 2 words: Ronald McDonald
- 3 words: Hatched, matched, and detached (born, married, died)
- 4 words: Ill bred, enough said!
- 5 words: Sermon was long, understood wrong!
- 6 words: Forget the bread? Eat crackers instead.
- 7 words: Wow those leaping lizards and crocodile gizzards
- 8 words: If you come late, you'll find a closed gate
- 9 words: Size of the tire? No, depth of the mire.
- 10 words: See, you don't have to write forever, to be clever!
- 11 words: You may spend lots of time finding words that will rhyme
- 12 words: This verse sounds awful to read, but it rhymes, it does, indeed.

This is rhyme in its simplest form and your rhyme patterns can grow and become more complex as your ability and interest in poetry grow. If you eventually find that you want to pursue some of the advanced, "serious technical" aspects of poetry, see the list of references for beginning poets on page _____.

Finding the Right Rhyme

Much of the sheer enjoyment of writing comes when you are looking for a rhyme. Let's say the word you need to rhyme is "rhyme" so you start jotting… dime… grime… time… lime… mime… prime… crime… slime… ahhh… ahhh, you run out, and so start… gime…hime… jime… kime… skime… tryme.. zyme… Now you need a rhyme for "June"— "moon" is the most popular, but that doesn't fit your poem and there are a million moon and June poems out there already . So down the list you go… goon… soon… loon… tune… spoon… boom... foon… scoon… woon…etc. Some of the variations you'll conceive will be so funny, you'll make yourself laugh.

In your desperation for a rhyme you'll come up with some crazy uninvented words, which you'll be tempted to use. Do it, at least every once in a while, if it turns you on or makes the verse better—the reader will think they just don't know the word!

Can't Find a Rhyme?

"Somewhere out there is the perfect word to rhyme with this, I just know it!"

You'll find yourself in this position often, even after you get really good. You can't find a rhyme, and for hours you'll be stalemated (or we might say "versecursed"). You may beat on yourself, invent odd words, chisel, cheat, sweat, and pray—all in all making a fun poem into a full-fledged semantic struggle. If you try and try, and can't seem to find anything to fit the flow:

1. Sleep on it.
2. Rearrange the line.
3. Add another word on the end.

Rhymes Don't Have to Be a Perfect Match

Sometimes there is just no word that rhymes perfectly and fits into the structure of the verse, or there may be certain ending words you simply want to use at the end of certain lines. When this happens, just get something that comes close to rhyming and it may work. It may even be a pleasant change from rigid "singsong" rhyming. If there is some harmony or similarity in the sound of the two words, it will often be good enough for the purpose and accomplish what you need. For an example of this, here is a poem I wrote on my work

shirt while a contractor was building a ballfield for me.

King Krogers

If you want some hours of pleasure
Something purely fun.
Go watch at a construction site
a father and two sons.

They call themselves "The Krogers"
and can really excavate.
Build up or tear down
Anything in this state.

They don't just own and run
every tractor that is made
These boys with big men's toys
are artists with the blade.

Accuracy within an inch
with twenty tons of steel
They can move a mountain of dirt
and never spin a wheel.

They bid fair, and are always there
to attack the toughest chasm.
And they do all their work
with constant enthusiasm.

You'll find them on the rigs, not in their
   truck
And you'll not meet better folk
Inventing special things they need
With dusty sketches in diesel smoke.

It's great to see good Americans
with all that work ambition
The Krogers are so dog-gone good
to watch them,
   we should charge
   admission.

—DA August 1997

Jerky rhyme?

Often when you write a poem and get every detail in it you want, rather than having a satisfying rhyme, it might break rhythm or be jerky.

It's like walking down the sidewalk trying not to step on the cracks: your stride seldom fits between the cracks perfectly, so you have to stretch or shorten your step every fifteen cracks or so, so your rhythm is jerky. You can feel this in a poem too and wonder if others notice it. They do!

For example:

> A glance in the closet, overstuffed, a sure
>   contact for staph
> And homework stuffed behind the shelf
>   could nearly make you laugh.

What is the solution?

You don't need to learn any complicated structure rules, but poetry read to yourself or others really should have a uniformity of rhythm, about the same number of beats per measure. In other words, the beat or bounce of the lines within a poem should match. So go back and read and re-read. If it doesn't flow or have a steady beat and seems jerky, you need to doctor it up a little.

> A look in the overstuffed closet, could give
>   you a case of staph
> The homework piled in the back, would
>   really make you laugh.

Here are some shorter lines with a jerky beat:

> The vacuum cleaner couldn't consume the
>   crud
> because of the big bunch of mud

Sometimes it takes a while to match the lines with the message.

> The poor vacuum was unable, to
>   consume all the crud,
> Nut and bolts and matchbox
>   cars, and big hunks of mud.

You can add words, change words, reverse order, eliminate words—anything to get it to swing.

Sometimes you'll come up with what seems like a perfect rhyme, but when you read it out loud there is a bumpy sound. The lines may rhyme but they just don't sound right. For example:

> Harry horsed the offending gate,
> Causing it to capitulate.

The reason is that "gate" is a single-syllable word and "capitulate" a four-syllable one. You need to be aware of this when you are rhyming.

One-syllable words: gate/mate, hat/cat, hot/trot

Two-syllable words: ten-der/bend-er, hawk-er/stalk-er

Three-syllable words: temp-ta-tion/e-la-tion

Four-syllable words: ca-pit-u-late/sub-stan-ti-ate

Sometimes words with different numbers of syllables will mix OK, but if you can't get a smooth flow, see if uneven syllables might be the problem. It will help to have others read the drafts of your poems to you. You can really spot the bumps then. You, the writer, know they are there and will compensate or compromise your enunciation to make the lines work, sound good. But others will read what they see!

Is It a Crime
If It Doesn't Rhyme?

I can remember well the day when it was someone's turn in class to read a poem and they read some lines of beauty, but none of those lines came even close to rhyming. I was baffled but the teacher nodded approvingly. At that moment I found out all poetry doesn't have to rhyme.

You've noticed all through this book that I've used rhyme in most of the things I've written. I guess it is my fourth-grade love for swinging the lines—it was so much easier to memorize and remember things when "candlestick" came marching after "Jack be nimble, Jack be quick." But some of us struggle so much with rhyming our message is lost in the process. All poetry doesn't have to rhyme—if necessary, you can just write in lines.

Non-rhyming poetry is more difficult to remember, thus its genius is sometimes overlooked. Rhythm and rhyme are fun for the reader or listener, and anything with a "beat" or rhyme is read or listened to more willingly, and I believe appreciated more. I've had some great, even classic, writing sent to me by beginners, poems with tremendous messages, profound statements, just in stanzas with no rhyme. Good as it is, it doesn't sing like rhyme does, and most people won't appreciate it as much. How many people would be singing or saying:

Hickory, dickory, dock, the mouse ran up
   the timepiece,
It pealed one and so he ran back down.

On the other hand, here is a sample of some of the lovely nonrhyming lines everyday people have sent me:

Heritage

Our kids were quick, elusive,
  like spilled mercury
and I chased them across the
  map
trying to gather them into a
  suburban mold.
They were like a string of
  giant firecrackers
and I womanned the hoses
praying there'd be something
  left
when the explosions stopped.

They served their seasons in
  Hell
and I tried to bribe Charon
to pole them back across the
  Styx
before that season ended.
They were alive to the world
in ways I've never been,
and they learn, oh they
  learned
what I will never know.

They produce. They interact.
  They excel.
They have some subtle powers
  of wisdom,
the patience of cold rolled
  steel,
the courage to tell the truth or
  be silent.
They were born agile and
  strong
to a woman who cannot run,
a banty hen with a brood of
  swimming ducks.
                 —Grace Longeneker

Great content and feeling! So if lack of rhyme is limiting your expression, forget it, you are still a bonafide poet. (See page 73 for more good examples of unrhymed poetry.)

NEED SOME HELP WITH RHYMING?

I've seen a lot of gadgets, charts, computer programs, and reference books made to help writers, and I imagine many of these have some value for shoring up and supporting a writer, pro or amateur. I myself own or have access to many "how to" and "help out" books and tools, including the library, but I often find myself writing at times and places where most such aids are not accessible or truly portable.

So what I carry along with me everywhere is a long yellow tablet, a pen, and a little wallet-size electronic thesaurus, my one "outside my own brain" tool. When you are looking for a rhyme or alliteration of some kind, would like a whole list of words to pick from (so you can find the one that best fits, instead of the one that first strikes your mind), you can't beat something like this for speed and quality.

Let me give a couple of examples here. I am writing along on a poem about the big examination and I've reached line three.

The Test

Tomorrow at ten (my
  teeth do clench)
I face the exam on a
  cold school bench.
I've studied all that
  might be asked

Now I need to find a rhyme with "asked," so I do what any rhymer would do, let's see… task… bask… masked…naskt… I try all I can think of, and even consider inventing a word or two of my own to come up with a rhyme. Too many poets get stuck here and force a rhyme or use a word that doesn't do the job well. What I need now is a choice … other ways or words to say "ask"… so in a second I can type into my little thesaurus ASK—hit Enter, then "S" for synonyms and out comes:

examine	solicit
inquire	demand
interrogate	call for
query	crave
question	necessitate
quiz	require
bespeak	take
desire	invite
request	bid

Now I have nineteen words I could use instead of "ask," including several more workable for my purpose, so now I can change the line in question to:

I've studied all that might be required,

Now I look at all the words that rhyme with "required"— tired, fired, mired, sired, hired. This gives me options for a fourth line like:

Until two A.M. when eyes were tired.
  or
So I'd be smart and never fired.
  or
To exclude the chance that I might get
  mired.
  or
To gain a skill that I may be hired.

A thesaurus is just a tool to open up avenues and options your mind often refuses to find. Let's say that as I get farther along in my poem I hit another snag:

> Then comes a question you know but can't recall
> Your brain goes on overload, into a stall

That's okay, but kind of hokey, this time I hit the word "stall" to see if there is a better word here and get:

> arrest
> check
> halt
> interrupt
> stay

Now I really like the word "arrest," it's kind of a surprise power word I'd never have thought of on my own, so that gives me a new idea:

> Then it comes, that one question in every test
> You know the answer, but your mind is in arrest.

A thesaurus just gives you a bigger palette, a wider range of shades and colors to paint the exact picture you have in mind. Those big old thesaurus books are great, but slow when it comes to finding things and huge to carry. My "Wordmaster" thesaurus is the size of a small calculator and it fits easily in pocket or purse.

And it has 144,000 options!

Rhyming Dictionaries

Another great aid for versifying are the more familiar rhyming dictionaries. Webster makes one that is a truly "traveling" size (*Webster's Compact Rhyming Dictionary*), and it's a nice sturdy little hardcover so it'll hold up to a lot of hard verse hunting. You may have to familiarize yourself first with the pronunciation symbols, which are explained at the front of the book, and for that matter in the front of any dictionary. You may need these to help find the right entry, because often word endings are pronounced a little differently, depending on what word they happen to be the ending of! But once you stop being intimidated by these simple symbols, you'll have a long and instant list of rhymes for the ending of any word right at your fingertips. (Beats just working your way down the alphabet looking for a rhyme, as we often do!)

CHAPTER SIX

Shorter is better,

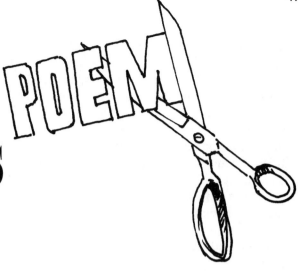

And Other Pointers for Poemcrafting

> Just how long should I make this verse?
> Methinks too long doth make it worse.

Where to start on a poem isn't half as critical as where to end. Think about this a minute—in all your life, how many long poems have you ever read that weren't assigned for a class or something? I'll bet very few. After the first page, I believe a poem loses about twenty percent of the reader's interest and endurance, and about that much more is lost, per page, as the reader keeps turning and reading. After five pages most of us are out of it mentally, because reading poetry is more demanding than reading plain old paragraphs. Even the great ones like Milton's "Paradise Lost," I find myself "wading" through after so long.

The shorter you can say something, the more of your verse you can keep to one page or less, the better it will be appreci-

ated. Most of that maximum impact verse, the verse we like and remember best—and call up and use often in our life—is the shorter verse.

For effective poetry, in general think short, unless your subject seems to demand fuller treatment. There are some subjects and styles that can get away with it, greats like "The Highwayman," and "Maud Muller," that can make you read eagerly through several pages and give you a fat reward at the end, but they better be good and be telling an exciting **story**. If you feel moved to write about a more abstract subject like the mystic qualities of the mosquitoes and mountains on a moonlit night, I'd keep it short. If a poem is fun enough and the story good enough, and describes a unique happening or a happening the reader is already interested in, it can get away with greater length and still be "right" to read.

Even then, however, you need to beware of those times when the verse just keeps rolling out after you've made your point. There is some value in doing a little "overkill" when you're on a roll, a few extra verses so that you'll have more to chose the best from. The problem is that after all that inspiration and work you'll probably be in love with them all, and keep them all in and ruin a perfectly good poem. Know when to cut it off and shut it down— enough is enough!

I have to fight this all the time. I have the idea or stimulus and a good start, I say what I wanted to say to entertain or impress...and then just keep pounding the idea to death, until a good half-page poem is three pages long. Read some of Ogden Nash's or Edwin Markham's stuff. They can give you four pages in four lines. Remember, more than ever, this is the age of impatience and short attention spans. People are much more likely to read and remember your work if IT ISN'T TOO LONG!

Beware of Trying to Be TOO POETIC AND PROFOUND

The original sin of writing poetry is trying too hard to be "a poet." Most of us have a memory of "Thanatopsis" and "Paradise Lost" humming around in our head somewhere, and when we sit down to write we make what ought to be a friendly letter into a formal business letter, you might say. We get wound up and lost in being poetic and profound, instead of writing something with a perky personality and a plain message that all can understand and enjoy.

Somewhere along the line, many of us seem to have absorbed the idea that "if it's indecipherable (cryptic, enigmatic, mystical-sounding) it must be poetic and profound." **Don't get too fancy, Nancy!**

Don't get so poetic you lose your point. If the reader has to use too much energy to find and draw out the meaning (because you've used so many big words and complicated constructions), they won't have any energy or patience left over to enjoy it.

If a big word and a little word can say the same thing, use the little one. The big word usually breaks the rhythm anyway or is mumbled over to get on to something the reader can pronounce. Remember that being down to earth is enough, in fact better. You don't need to be six feet under, with your meaning buried under multiple layers of images, allusions, and symbols that few can decode or decipher. Try your verses out on an eight-year-old and if they grin, you've got something going. If they wrinkle their forehead, you've probably failed.

Making It Funny: humor in poetry

I've never read or heard a poem that broke anyone into hysterical laughter, so if yours don't or won't, relax. Even the best "funny poets" get only a conservative (or perhaps silent) chuckle. Getting a simple grin is good going, a sudden smile from a reader is great acknowledgment. Some clapping and even one person asking for "a copy" means you have achieved some home-hitting humor.

Don't strain to make up something funny in a poem, writing a poem about a funny situation is easier. Remember, **humor comes from incongruity**—that is, you are expecting a person approaching a door to open the door and go through. If, however, he can't get it open or runs into it or the doorknob comes off, people start to giggle and laugh. What's happening is different from what was supposed to happen, or we imagined would happen— the more incongruous, the more the watchers or readers howl.

Here is a quick corny example:

I kissed my wife,
Her quiet hand
As I was leaving
For a distant land.

versus:

I kissed my wife
Her quiet hand
And snagged my lip
On the wedding band.

A clever poem about real happenings with a humorous side is always funny. The CEO of my cleaning company, Arlo Luke, a dignified executive, dead tired from twelve hours of meetings and an eight-hour flight, landed at the L.A. Airport once and hit the restroom… in error. It was the women's restroom, and once in the stall, seeing high heels he knew and so he waited until the room seemed empty and then bolted for the door. He scared a woman out of her wits; she reported him as a would-be molester and the result was an all-points-bulletin police search for Arlo. The story got out and at the next company meeting, the gifted Mark Browning (see page 51)

penned this verse which was read to the entire management staff, all ninety of us, bringing many roars of approval.

Heels clicked on the floor as she came in the door,
It put his poor head in a swoon;
A peek out the stall confirmed it all,
He's enthroned in the ladies room.

Waiting his chance and stealing a glance,
He dashed from the cursed place;
And fairly ran over the security rover,
Coming in to fix up her face.

The legs were old, but his heart was bold,
So he dashed up the stairs in a fright;
"Lost her" he chuckled, as his knees almost buckled,
And he flopped down to wait for his flight.

But soon cops on task, had questions to ask:
Perverted or honest mistake?
It's a relief to know that our bold CEO
While forgetful, at least ain't a flake.

Another safe bet, when it comes to humor in poetry, is poems in which we poke fun at ourselves. Readers are always ready to smile at commentary of this kind, and they may enjoy it so much they don't quite realize it may actually be poking fun at us all. A good little example of this (one of those "author unknown" poems that crop up here, there, and everywhere):

A Reluctant Investor's Lament

I hesitate to make a list
of all the countless deals I've
missed.
Bonanzas that were in my grip—
I watched them through my
fingers slip.
The windfalls which they should
have brought
were lost because I overthought.
I thought of this, I thought of
that,
I could have sworn I smelled a
rat.
And while I thought things over
twice,
Another grabbed them at the
price.
It seems I always hesitate,
then make up my mind too late.
A very cautious man am I
And that is why I never buy.

A corner here, then acres there,
compounding values year by
year.
I chose to think and as I thought
Others bought the deals I
should have bought.
The golden chances I had then
Are lost and will not come again.

Today I cannot be enticed,
For everything's so overpriced.
The deals of yesteryear are
dead;
The market's soft—*and so's my
head!*

Last night I had a fearful dream,
I know I wakened with a
scream.
Some Indians approached my
bed,
for trinkets on the barrel-head.
For dollar bills numb'ring
twenty-four,
nothing less and nothing more,
they'd sell Manhattan Isle to
me...
the most I'd go was twenty-
three.
The red men scowled:
  "Not on a bet!"
And sold to Peter Minuit.
At times a teardrop drowns my
eye
For deals I had, but did not buy.
And now life's saddest words I
pen—
"If only I'd invested then!"
—Author unknown, submitted
by E. B. Beard

Those Fortunate Few Who Can Write Fast and Well

Anyone can write poetry, poems and verses, but some people seem to be able to write it faster than the rest of us.

I labor at many of my poems, while a friend of mine, who has been a business partner for more forty years now, seems to do it as naturally as breathing. In a few minutes of scribbling he can knock out a verse, flawless and funny. It used to unnerve me how he could do that, but he could.

One day, for example, one of his small children's pets, a gerbil, died. While everyone else was standing around scratching their heads over it or bewailing it, Mark jotted out the following:

Who Killed Fred?

Hang our head, Fred is dead.
Ashes and sackcloth, poor,
    poor Fred.
What a nothing life he
    led—
Dime store chips and last
    week's Post,
Wilted lettuce, dehydrated
    toast.
Small wonder he should yield the
    ghost.
Hang our head.
                            —Mark Browning

I love that verse and have kept it all these years. Every time I read it I chuckle at its clever and accurate summary of a gerbil's existence (some humans' lives come pretty close, huh?)

You're bound to meet some first-draft geniuses during your life, writers whose work seems to be born perfect. Don't judge yourself or your work by comparison, or worry if you need take longer to write and polish. If you see one of these folks at work just saw "Wow" and spend a little more time at your writing and before you know it you may be just as deft.

Mark's ability just makes me love verse more, inspires me to write more, to be as good as he is. Mark doesn't write all that much as far as I know (maybe secretly), but he could take the afternoon off and crank out a couple of dozen masterpieces and not even get excited. The good news is there are lots of you "Marks" out there who have never even written a line—you can and **should**!

A Different Way to Write a Poem

All of us question behavior and ethics constantly, in almost every situation we encounter, many times a day. Sometimes we even wrestle with it in our dreams. Remember to write them down, those feelings, puzzlements, or frustrations, injustices, or solutions that might hit you in the shower, when you're daydreaming, raking the leaves, or even reading or watching TV. Your mind, processing experiences, will produce tons of poem fodder for you.

Let's look at an example of how this comes about.

On a 500-mile ride home from Seattle once, I was pondering the fact that life confronts us daily with decisions that pit our discipline against powerful forces like greed, anger, laziness, the desire for revenge, sexual drives, and hunger. Keeping on the committed side of the line is hard, because that "I want to" is always there, requiring a constant arbitration within us, to do the right things for the right reason. Resistance to temptation can become a grind and thrashing this over that afternoon, it hit me that maybe, just maybe, yearning and yearning and yearning for something that is against your ethics might be more damaging than yielding.

For instance:

1. We've wanted for forty-two years to put down that obnoxious relative (he deserves it, too), but instead we've been nice.

2. Every day for twenty-five years, we've wanted to tell off that petty official we have to deal with who has intimidated us all this time. But instead we smile and express our grievances out of sight.

3. We've wanted to own that yacht our neighbor has for all of the twenty years he's had it, thought of little else in our spare time.

4. George's wife looks about as good to us as that yacht, and we've thought about that too for as many years, but remain a gentleman.

5. We've wanted to ram our car through those insulting barrier gates at the toll station, but never have.

6. Etc.

Being a moral person like we all are, we didn't do any of these things, because of the negative consequences that would probably follow. However for years and years, these desires have bugged us daily, occupied our mind, causing inner struggle, daydreaming, a drain of our energy and emotions, even our financial resources.

Surely that constant yearning, nonstop for decades, has done and is doing some damage. Maybe stepping on the gas and tearing one of those striped arms to shreds, getting fined $150.00 and paying it and getting it over with, would satisfy us. One session of well-chosen insults directed at Cousin Pete long ago would have saved thirty years of frustration and wanting to. And we'd be free of all those smoldering thoughts, they'd be out of our system. Things like this might be a good way to get on with life, and eliminate that pounding on our subconscious forever.

Thinking about this I jotted the thought down on a pad as I sat there in the driver's seat: a good concept to give a speech on, teach a lesson on, or even WRITE A POEM ON!

The thing that pushed me over the edge on this particular poem idea, and gave me another format for writing poems, came ten years later. (And no, I hadn't bought the yacht from George or his wife in the deal, nor had I said a nasty word to that court clerk I'm still dealing with. Something happened to made me write a poem on it.)

I was at the airport one day, an hour early like they tell you to be, and I'd picked a booklet of local real estate listings out of the "Welcome to Pocatello" literature stand. It was full of the kinds of places every person yearns for: acreage with snowcapped mountain views, clear streams with trout jumping, tall pines and poplars with wind rushing through them, small peach and cherry orchards, quaint log houses rich with history, plenty of space for the kids to play, cattle grazing and deer wandering in the background, at least thirty kinds of songbirds and waterbirds. Plus easy payments!

That little book was full of deals on places of beauty that we've all dreamed of someday owning. I was practically salivating as I devoured the ads, mentally doing some financial maneuvers to fit the most delectable of these into my life. There had to be the perfect one in all of these just for me! I wasn't just yearning for, I was seriously considering owning some more land.

Then reality snapped me out of it. I felt totally ridiculous and asked myself, "What in the world am I doing drooling over this utopian real estate in the mountains of the west, when I already have a sixty-five acre ranch with one of the best views in Idaho, twenty fresh springs complete with watercress, all kinds of wildflowers and birds, wild geese, foxes, and fish, pines and junipers, a 6500 square foot mansion that overlooks a beautiful green valley with a meandering stream and 9,000-foot mountains on either side, miles of gleaming white fence, a giant workshop with welders and tractors, a garden with soil equal to any on earth—probably the nicest place in Southern Idaho, and I already owned it. And not only that, in Hawaii, on the garden island, Kauai, right where they filmed *South Pacific* and *Jurassic Park*, I already own, debt free, a five-acre jungle estate with one of the nicest new homes on the island. There are spectacular flowers and exotic plants everywhere, the best neighbors you could have, and a workshop there too! Am I crazy to be sitting there sighing over a collection of classified ads for things and places that could hardly outdo what I already have? There's one word for this—stupid! But the reality was that I was just yearning for something other than what I had, as we all do every single day.

I started a poem right then, writing on a trip as I often do, composing two-line stanzas at random, and later putting them together and adjusting them. However I couldn't seem to make this particular idea work; couldn't draft it, as I had hundreds of others, in minutes.

So I did a completely different thing, and it might give you an idea for an easier, more effective start.

First I took the two key words here, "yearn" and "yield," put a line after each of them, and listed below it all the synonyms in my thesaurus for each of these:

YEARN	YIELD
long	buckle under
ache	capitulate
crave	cave
dream	defer
hanker	knuckle under
hunger	submit
itch	bend
lust	break
pine	collapse
sigh	crumple
thirst	fold up
	waive
	surrender
	leave
	lay down
	abandon
	relinquish
	succumb

You can see that a lot of ammo had suddenly appeared for a poem, all the different ways of expressing these thoughts. But still I didn't start writing stanza or verse, but went down the list, and added some one-word rhymes, one or two or whatever came to mind.

YEARN	**YIELD**
long/wrong	buckle under/blunder
ache/take	capitulate/captivate
crave/slave	cave/stave
dream/cream	defer/endure
hanker/canker,	knuckle under/buckle
conquer	submit/wit
hunger/younger	bend/lent
itch/snitch	break/take
lust/bust, dust,	collapse/straps
must	crumple/tumble
pine/sign	fold up/cup
sigh/sky	waive/slave
thirst/burst	surrender/blender, tender
	leave/grieve
	lay down/clown
	abandon
	relinquish
	succumb/dumb

Then, instead of trying to write the whole poem from start to finish, I just did a bunch of two-line stanzas on the subject, using my list of rhyming words. Once I started into the poem, I didn't even use many of the words on the list—other words came to me.

Here are a few examples from my draft:

For forty years I've held
it back
The passion of suppressed
attack.

Ah yield, then put it in the past
Then I'll be free, perhaps, at
last.

To sigh, resist temptation's
song
A body knows when
something's wrong.

I wrote pages of these two-line verses and some of them started coming out pretty good. But when I put them together, it made a long, drawn out "moral struggle" verse, so I decided—something I had never done before—to divide the poem into three sections. The end result? Well, judge for yourself.

What's the wisest of the two "Y's"?

The Revolution

Too long we yearn and anticipate
Venturing past temptation's gate.

We scheme and dream and fantasize,
across the boundaries, about that other
prize.

For forty years we're held it back
the passion of suppressed attack.

Just once we'd like to sin and scoff
Exercise some hate and "tell 'em off."

Let loose, give up, and really purge,
and satisfy that long-banked urge.

Pounce and grab, and then move on—
we've stayed in bounds for way too long.

To the sensual and wicked, we'd like to bow
Obey the prod for pleasure **now.**

Instead of suffering that problem dream
And always whispering about missed cream.

II. The Rationale

Well, surely if we satisfy
Just once, what's tempted you and I.

Out of our system it would be
And we could settle into a better "me."

Longing and lust can surely canker
So doing it should dissolve the hanker.

For maybe this itch and endless pine
Is warping the very strength of my spine.

If a want or desire cannot be slaked
Maybe one sharp pain would beat an ache?

If I yield and then put it in the past,
Perhaps I will be free at last.

Unshackled from this forbidden thing,
Relieved indeed from a lifelong sting.

III. The Re-Resolve

Ah, true, the unfulfilled does have its
  thorns,
and virgin conduct can merit scorn.

But I know that once I'm through that door
with its long-awaited plunder, I'll just want
  more.

For getting all those forbidden toys
History tells us, just destroys.

The consequences, when we submit,
are more than it says in the holy writ.

Yet more yearning comes with "capitulate"
Many ugly rewards are the crumbler's fate.

Wisdom confirms 'twould be a blunder,
to bend, to break, and to buckle under.

Give up? Abandon? Progress lost?
Guess who will pay the waiver's cost?

For once in the pot with what you've
  yearned
A great lesson will you have learned.

When yielding gets you by the hand.
You'll yearn for freedom from no man's
  land.

Keep on Writing and You'll Get Better

I'm sure one of my loyal employees, Robert Knox, won't mind being used here as an example for the benefit of all of we poets. Several years ago poems started appearing on my desk from someone in the Northern Idaho District of my cleaning company. They were easily identifiable as beginner's work and not just one arrived here and there—this guy could write a poem about anything... and did. The whole world to him was "poem worthy"—he would write about nature, toilets, coworkers, cars, and chemicals. An encouraging comment from others or a poem appearing in our company newsletter only inspired him to increase production. Then came volumes, yes volumes, whole notebooks of them! Series I and Series II of his poems bound and copyrighted and dedicated to me and the other chief executives of my company.

Robert wrote so much and so many I scheduled in some time to read them as a courtesy, not always admiring the poems themselves as much as the awesome versifying drive Robert had. Robert told me he'd been an orphan and never knew the real meaning of love until he was eighteen. Now married to someone he cherished and working at a job he did well. Robert loved life and kept writing and writing and writing. One day, I received another of many "thanks for the job" letters from him and of course, a few poems were attached. The first of these was titled "The Old Mop," and reading it, I felt even a deeper respect and admiration for this young man. The poem was good, the other two with it were good too, because over the years he did two things:

1. Didn't just stop with his first few attempts, and just sit back and admire them forever after.
2. Kept writing... LOTS

Thanks to the material he poured out in assembly-line proportion, Robert developed into a first-class poet. He seasoned himself and gained feeling, rhythm, cadence, and value. Here is one of his recent efforts, for example.

That's Woman's Work

As a small child
So young and naive
Some things were taught
And some I believed.

Such as: Boys must always
keep feeling inside.
Heartfelt emotions
Must always hide.

And definitely don't
Let tenderness show,
Or wear an apron,
Cook, or sew.

Wash dirty dishes,
Do household chores,
Play with dolls,
Or scrub the floors.

Now that I'm older,
Hopefully with good sense,
I find this list
Is mostly nonsense.

I'll now make a list
Of things I now do;
And I'll be proud
To share it with you.

No lipstick I'll wear,
Nor yet wear pink,
But I sure can shine
A dirty, grubby sink.

Wash dirty dishes,
Launder the clothes,

Even dirty shorts
And wife's pantyhose.

I push a mean broom,
Mop floors anywhere,
Take out the garbage,
And polish silverware.

I'll darn the socks,
Iron and sew,
Push the vacuum,
And make bread dough.

Yes, cook and clean
At every given chance.
Even wait to be asked
By a lady to dance.

Though I can't play
With pretty dolls still
Holding a cute baby
Can be quite a thrill.

It's taken so long
To get over what's taught,
And do the things
That every man ought!

—Robert L. Knox

May we poets all learn from Robert—keep writing! Some day your first work (that one you worshipped) will look "first grade" to you. That's okay, because we progress from the first grade to the second, the fifth, and the eighth, and so on. Before you know it, you'll be putting out material that others love as much as you do!

How Much Our Poetry Means to Us

The attachment of poetry to our very soul is clearly revealed if you just watch the reaction of the author when a poem is read in public, lost, or criticized. It is almost humorous to see a full-grown adult (with business, family, community, even national ranking and responsibilities) leap to correct a single missed phrase or mispronounced syllable.

I remember once writing a great poem—at least I thought it was great—and leaving it for my production manager to type up. I returned to the office ten days later and in the pile of mail, typed letters and reports, and copies on my desk I found my brilliant poem, typed *in a paragraph!* Boy was that an insult, a smart woman like her didn't even recognize its magnificent rhythm as a poem. That same day I got word of a $120,000 profit in my cleaning company for the month, eight new contracts we'd been awarded, two requests for national television show appearances, and a physical exam report from my doctor pronouncing me in teenage condition. But none of this good news could offset getting my poem typed in a paragraph instead of stanzas—it bothered me all night.

Another time I came into the office looking for two little lines of verse I'd written a few days before and hadn't found typed up yet, and now I couldn't find the rough. As I was searching through the office, my CPA told me my company's 401K program was in the red $5,000, one branch of our operation had lost $61,000 this quarter, the Worker's Compensation laws in California had changed in a way that would mean an additional small fortune to be paid out by us, and other momentous and important news, to all of which I said, "Okay, okay, okay..." and nodded. Finally in desperation I moaned, "Now where IS that two-line poem I wrote...???"

I'm sure you could come up with equally dramatic examples from your own experience. Don't ever tell me our personal verse isn't dear to us!

Don't Let Those Precious Lines Be Lost!

A few years ago I was a public health officer at the National Boy Scout Jamboree and for some reason we staff members got to writing poems back and forth to each other and reading them aloud in the evening. The members of the commissary, the medical tent, and the latrine crew, all of us were firing little verses at each other. Man, was it fun, all of us working away, trying to come up with the best poem to get the best laugh.

We had a vibrant Catholic chaplain, Father Roger LaChance, who was the spirit of fun of our staff of leaders. I did a few lines in our "theme song" about his white legs (in swim trunks) that brought the tent down with laughter and applause. It was one of those once-a-year bits of luck when it comes to wording and rhyming, but I can't tell you exactly how it went. We were camped far from any copying machine and somebody borrowed the poem and it never came to light again—it is gone.

Make copies and keep what you write, **never** give your original away, it will bother you till your dying day!

I can't say enough about making copies of your poems, plenty of them, and even putting copies in three or a half-dozen different places or files. There is nothing worse than losing something that was one of your more ingenious moments.

> Always make and save
> some copies!

Keeping the "gonna writes"

You will have plenty of ideas for poems you want to write, or that need writing. You may even get a line or two start on some of these, but time, mood, or circumstance prevents you from finishing them now. Later is fine and sometimes even better. Just don't lose your idea or even the one line you have so far. I carry a little list with me in a notebook and just add to it as I go along. I flip it open, add my latest inspiration, or write one of the poems on there and cross it off. Here is what my August 97 list looked like:

5. Do a poem on being down—a little down (from a small setback or inconvenience), regular down (you're having a bad day), big-time down (real depression, with no end in sight, no use in going on).

6. Do a poem on Walt Disney:
To the list of "greatests" that have
ever lived
Measured for their portion given.
To bring a spark of decency
into the lives of you and me.
(finish someday)

7. Do a poem posing the problem: "If right is so good, so rewarding, why is it a struggle to do right? Or is it a struggle? It really is tougher to do evil, trouble is a burden— ugly and inefficient, and it strains our life." That is a pretty heavy subject but it could make a good serious poem.

1. Do poem on getting ready, prepared.

2. Do a poem on: Marching when miserable, Treading when tired. Walking when wounded. Working when you're not in the mood.

3. Do a poem on sandbagging—a river or in politics.

4. Do a poem on "doing time" when you're not in jail. Make it clear that it's no different from doing time in jail.

8. Do a poem on "the mean streak." My dad used to say about some horses we had, "that one has a mean streak." Years later as I worked around different people, I'd meet some truly hostile ones, and the thought popped into my head that some people were like those horses, they had a mean streak. I carry this idea around with me on my list and someday I'll do it—this is a subject that has some substance to draw on.
9. Do a poem on our tendency to look for improvements from an external source, rather than internally, where they have to come from. ("If all drugs were eliminated, we'd have half the crimes and divorces... etc.")
10. Do a poem on "Spousegoat" (rough start)

I'm glad to have a wife
to blame my woes upon.
All the aches and pains of life
and other things that go wrong.

Could she have caused my cholesterol,
with that cooking divine?
Who loses all my tools
and causes me to whine?

Who causes me to be late for work?

(she mis-set the alarm)
Who makes the bed so warm and cozy,
and twists my very arm?

Her fault it is, when the gas mileage goes
  down
And why does she spend so much money
running my errands in town?
It's her, it's her, I often think
Who causes all my belts to shrink!
(Get list of other "blamers" and finish)

Poems and ideas, where do they come from?

We probably have at least a half dozen poem opportunities a day, some days several dozen. We need to recognize and capture them!

HOW MANY POEMS SHOULD YOU WRITE?

How many poems should or must you write? Well… one is better than nothing and if you only do one good one all your life, that is more of an accomplishment than those many people out there who wish they'd done one. Two is twice as good and four is twice as good as that. But you don't write poems to keep count or see how big a pile you can amass, you write them because you feel like it and as they are called for by the events of your life.

These days I generally do about one a week, unless it's an overloaded week that distracts from my hobby. That is about fifty a year to handle and file and read or share. If you and I only wrote one a month, in twenty years we'd have 240 great poems… **enough for a book,** no less. If you only write one good poem every year, by retirement, you'll already have forty good ones done! Once, when I was on a cruise for a couple of days in Alaska, I wrote six or seven a day, good ones too, and then didn't write another for three or four months.

Don't try to schedule verse, but do learn to grab it when it goes by or through you.

Refining your lines

You'll be even prouder when you polish your poetry a little. "Touchup" only takes a tiny bit of time from you (and maybe the friend you use as your sounding board or "second opinion"). Here are some of the "red flags" you'll want to watch for, when you're refining your lines.

Don't Let Your Poems Be Too Predictable

Back in the days of "the ultimate stereo," my brother-in-law picked me up a professional-quality reel-to-reel tape unit and then copied onto some two hours of reel absolutely the best classics, songs and instrumentals. I was overwhelmed and gratefully thanking him, when he served me a caution: "The only thing wrong with this, having all the best together, is that you will unconsciously memorize the order and soon start to anticipate and wait for what is coming next, instead of savoring what is playing." After a few months of playing I discovered that by gosh he was right! Out

of hundreds of songs I knew what was "next" and worried and waited and geared for it, almost tuning out the present beauty—really strange.

A few years ago, watching TV, I started saying the next lines of a sitcom program before the actor could. "You've seen it before" my wife would say. No way, I hadn't either, the sitcom attempts at comedy follow such a sure pattern it was easily predictable, almost figured itself out! Again this cuts enjoyment because you find yourself working ahead and missing the present, so I never bother to watch them anymore.

Don't conversations with people we know well get to be that way, too? We'll absorb and predict their pattern so well subconsciously we can almost take over their side of the conversation. I believe this is one reason some marriages fail—predictability—we're so bored with the overall pattern we miss what is being felt and going on at the present.

Poems are really vulnerable to this. If

someone is reading along and the verse pattern so rigid and rhyme so apparent, the reader can often say the next line without even reading it.

*It was a soft romantic night in **June**.* Now we just know the next verse is going to end with a gorgeous or haunting moon. Or when we hear *Lizzie Borden took an ax,* we are already filling in how many *"whacks."* This is predictability. Beginners especially fall into this when producing poetry. We use the immediate and obvious, the same thought and rhyme the reader does, so our poems aren't very fresh, interesting, or surprising.

So after that:

It was a soft romantic night in June,

hit the reader with something like:

The ice cream melted, they had no spoon.

Or:

Lizzie Borden took an ax,
to divide her children's four Big Macs.

A little "off-the-wall" keeps the reader or listener guessing, from anticipating it all.

Another way to avoid predictability is to reverse your lines, and put your power and punch line on the second (last) line, not on the first where it seems to go. This will keep the reader or listener poised and unable to predict the outcome.

DO THIS

From a loose saddle going round and round
Harry's butt was now on the ground.

NOT THIS

Harry's butt was now on the ground
From a loose saddle going round and round.

"Leaning" to Aid the Meaning

Have you ever seen a Christmas tree that toted too many trinkets? Remove a few dozen and it improves the tree dramatically. Apply this de-trinketing to your verse, too—we think of a poem as such special writing we often tend to overdecorate it. Here is a short verse I jotted down after seeing a commercial on TV for those pathetic starving youngsters somewhere "over there."

From **the** other countries across the sea
For food we **all** hear a constant plea.
Bulging tummies **and** haunting eyes
Some charity to silence the cries.
That we might fill **all** those empty bowls
With nourishment for **those** fasting souls.
At home, **too,** I wonder with some dread
About our own kids so fair and fed.
Hungry still, their vessels **are** bare
And hearts aching for some parent's care.

All cries are silenced with **lovely** toys and stuff
Playskool, TV seems **like** quite enough.
While **those** selfish parents **do** play and flaunt
Our youth too are **so** starved and gaunt.
Compassion! Help! A worthy <u>roam</u>
To cure **our** world hunger, start at home.

This got the message across, but I've learned to go back over a poem and see how many words (especially the little ones like "and," "the," "so," "of," etc.) I can yank out for a trimmer, neater, more concise message. I took fourteen trinkets out of this poem, the words in boldface below.

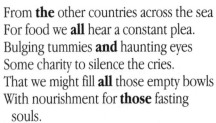

From **the** other countries across the sea
For food we **all** hear a constant plea.
Bulging tummies **and** haunting eyes
Some charity to silence the cries.
That we might fill **all** those empty bowls
With nourishment for **those** fasting
 souls.
At home, **too,** I wonder with some dread
About our own kids so fair and fed.
Hungry still, their vessels **are** bare
And hearts aching for some parent's
 care.

All cries are silenced with **lovely** toys and
 stuff
Playskool, TV seems **like** quite enough.
While **those** selfish parents **do** play and
 flaunt
Our youth too are **so** starved and gaunt.
Compassion! Help! A worthy <u>roam</u>
To cure **our** world hunger, start at home.

Now read the final version, and see if
you don't agree that it reads better:

From other countries across the sea
For food we hear a constant plea.
Bulging tummies, haunting eyes
Some charity to silence the cries.
That we might fill those empty bowls
With nourishment for fasting souls.
At home, I wonder with some dread
About our own kids so fair and fed
Hungry still, their vessels bare
Hearts aching for some parent's care.

All cries are silenced with toys and stuff
Playskool, TV seem quite enough.
While selfish parents play and flaunt
Our youth too are starved and gaunt.
Compassion! Help! No need to roam.
To cure world hunger, start at HOME.

What Can You Eliminate and Still Convey the Message?

Some people love to hear themselves talk, and some of us love to hear ourselves rhyme...so we go on and on and on in a poem, wearing the reader (or a good idea) into drowsiness. I once labored over a poem about my feelings concerning real estate ownership, and I finally had four solid stanzas. Then I did what we all should do with our verses—read them to decide what we can eliminate and still convey the message. I eliminated three of the four stanzas and had the whole message:

> I don't want to control or own
> Any "lifeless" real estate.
> Inactive properties to me
> Is living second rate.

Now here, since I'm sure you're wondering, is the original version:

My Real Estate Code

Some lands and buildings we do need
to earn and live at ease
at home or workplace, owned or rented,
land and structure should serve to please.

To under-use or over-tend
seems a waste indeed,
to hold and fence land's use away
insults the virtue "need."

I don't want to control or own
any "lifeless" real estate.
Inactive properties to me
is living second rate.

I always want my deeded share
to have direction and goals to give,
I want the course that they display
to help me not exist but live.
—DA, 1994

Most of our verse will be focused on a subject, one subject, and we usually have a tendency to "over-treat it and repeat it." That is fine WHILE you're writing.

But when you finally get your poem roughed out in its entirety, it is wise to go back and see which lines are the most essential. You don't need to say the same thing five different ways, unless showing the many different ways we can say something happens to be the actual subject of your poem. You'll usually find that out of eight or ten stanzas, you can switch and shorten and strike out and end up with a nice precise six or seven stanzas (which will fit nicely all on one side of one page).

Fixing Those Weak Spots

During the all-out effort of writing some verse, we can get pretty desperate to make a fit, and when nothing comes forth after we've been at it for a couple of hours, we'll use the best we can come up with at the time. Because we are worn down and eager to be done with it, when we finish the poem sounds good.

But re-reading it later (after a rest to regain objectivity), out pops a part of it that just isn't up to snuff—it's too glib, trite, clichéd, contrived, even downright corny or sappy. We recognize this well because we've seen it in other amateur poems, often in only one or two lines of the entire poem. The biggest offenders here are usually the result of using a word that rhymes but doesn't fit or make sense or say it just right.

Ode to Ed

Oh Uncle Ed we loved so dear
Why he could kill a case of beer!
Born and raised on a dairy farm
He could do pushups with one arm.
He could yodel, he could sing
And fly the highest on the front yard swing.
He gave us money, he gave us time
He was much sweeter than a lime.

Now look how fake or forced that last line sounds—it lost Uncle Ed's personality. One weak spot like this can ruin an entire poem. How would I fix this?

He gave us money, he played with us.
Gee Uncle Ed was a great old cuss!

Again and again, until it sounds right!

You may find yourself with a pretty darn good piece of work, a poem you like so much you'll tolerate a glitch or two in it. You may eventually come to believe it doesn't matter. But it does.

When a poem of yours has problem spots, don't wring your brain in agony over it. Just read it over (and over if necessary, and out loud if possible). Anywhere it doesn't flow or doesn't seem to go, circle it with your pencil. This is kind of like locating the buried body or telephone line.

Then let the poem rest an hour or day or two. I've let some rest a year or two and then one day, when I'm using the poem in a talk or copying it for someone, I slap myself on the forehead! I've found a better word or order, and now it really is nice.

Just remember, when you read your poem over, to be honest and don't cheat when it comes to the sound or meaning. Read it "as is" so that an uneven flow, bad rhythm, or any word glitches will show up. This is the only way you'll ever be able to (or want to) change or improve your verses. Remember: if even an excellent poem has one bad rhyme or line, readers or listeners will focus on them and miss the rest of your masterpiece.

Some good ways to fix those bad spots:

- Stretch yourself a little further and find a different rhyme.
- Find a synonym for the ending word that says the same thing with a different sound.
- Reverse the sentence—put the last word first and the first last.
- Go to rhymes every third or fourth line instead of every other.

    Anything goes, just don't accept mediocrity when you are aware of it.

The more you write, the better you will get, and the less redos your poems will need after they have been drafted. Even without a teacher you will absorb the lessons of the past and self-educate yourself like painters and other artists do.

Stuck, Stymied, and a Little Discouraged?

When we're working over a poem and it just won't come out right, sometimes we sweat, strain, and beat ourselves up over it, and still it sounds awful. We're about to decide we aren't a poet at all, we're almost at Giveupville.

The next time this happens to you, stop everything and tune into a couple of the local country and western stations for an hour or two. Just listen to the songs—the words, the content, and the rhyming of the lyrics. I promise that after an hour of this, your stuff will suddenly look pretty darn good.

You'll be amazed at what a country lyricist can do with just three rhyming words: you, blue, and through. Some of the verse big-time "artists" get away with is astonishing, and the sums they get paid for it are astounding.

I don't mean any offense to you folks who only like two kinds of music: country, and western. I play the guitar and once knew (and sang and yodeled) all four verses of every Hank Williams song!

Leave It Alone or Till Later If...

Sometimes, no matter how fast our heart is beating, our brain and fingers just can't manage to convert into verse what we feel and want to say. Even if we are in love with the concept. We slap our forehead, bend pens into bananas, put the thesaurus on overload, and still all we have is corny, preachy pap.

We all have our lesser efforts, weak verses, false starts, and utter failures… we've put plenty of work into those babies, too, but nothing worthwhile seems to come forth. The idea is good, the need is there, but over and over the result falls short. Or you can't get your brain to turn over, not even once, you are in "suspension of stanzas"….**join the crowd!**

I'll bet if we could see the pile of starts and stops, the crumpled pages, the failures, unsuccessful attempts, and unfinished poems of the great ones (Longfellow and the like) we would not be appalled, just assured that every poem we start isn't going to get finished. At least not right now.

> This stinks,
> methinks.
>
> One thing that can really dampen your enthusiasm for poem writing is getting stuck on a verse, subject, or rhyme that just won't go anywhere. It can make you mad at it, yourself, and the world. So I suggest: "Give up on it." Not poetry, just that particular project for a while.

I work too hard on my poems to wad them up and toss them in a wastebasket, so I made a file called The Great File of Unfinished. This is where the real stumpers go, the ones that seem to have a serious case of blockage. I carry some of these with me in a little folder called Poems to Develop, Heal, and Rescue. Many of these eventually find their way back to the unfinished (failure) pile. I'll bet even the best poet's failure file is thicker than their finished and polished pile. So don't let it bother you, no one posts their failures out for all to see. If you keep those problematic poems in the "low pulse" drawer long enough, with a little age and experience and some revelation and growth, you may be able to pull them out and pull off a really good one. Toss your page of pondering in a file and let it go for a while— maybe permanently!

Don't abandon your original feelings and ideas when you are doing this, however. They are unique and often your first instincts to write about something are the best you'll ever have. Just because you can't formulate it eloquently yet doesn't mean anything is wrong. There has got to be a poem in the "the value of a made bed," for example. For years I've pondered and reasoned and studied on the question of why a made bed has such a great impact on the mental and emotional well-being of we humans. I've come up with nothing to quite do justice to the subject yet (and you probably are thinking "I can see why"). But I'm convinced that someday the sheet will drop neatly onto my mind's mattress and I'll do one. So just watch, should you live that long!

Keep your attempts and notes on poems like this in an envelope in the file with the idea (and the title, if you have one) on the envelope. Some day at the right moment fact and fiction on the subject will flood your mind and you'll be able to get the rest of the way. I labored over a poem titled "A Team of Doctors" once, it went on and on with great insights on the medical profession. It is still in my failure (or temporary inanity) file. I chuckle reading the last two lines of the draft years later.

> That's why a penniless people we become
> Gads! Why is this poem so dumb!

I've got one in the failure file, a couple of pages full of scribbles and lines. I was pushing so hard on the pen it was cutting through the paper. The title was "The Intolerable Public" (probably a good one to keep in the failure file, huh?) The first two lines went...

There are sneezers, snoop-
ers, slammers, and sniffers
belchers, blowers, butt-ins,
and biffers…

It's sat there now for twelve years and I don't think it will ever turn into a master-piece awaited anxiously by anyone.

Likewise, I remember once being deeply impressed with an old woman who had eyes that sparkled with kindness. My romantical cells clamored to verse. I titled the poem "Kindly Eyes" worked and worked on it and still today have nothing.

Another time politics (I was the high paid keynote speaker) demanded that I attend a cocktail party prior to a conven-tion activity. I despise smoke, alcohol, and chatter and so to soothe my unease I decided to do a poem examining the merits of such a gathering. Boy is there poet ammo at these assemblies—people loose and loud make for all sorts of intrigue and outcomes. Yet even my best mood and skills never did come up with anything worthy of reading. So in this case too, I tossed the pages of trial and error into the Unfinished File. Drop whatever drowsys you—there's plenty more and better.

I have more than a hundred finished poems, but at last count at least sixty absolutely brilliant, badly needed poems (my estimation of them at the beginning) that are still in bits and scraps, some almost finished like the one below. This came to my mind after I stayed in five hotels in a row that were so fancy they were almost unusable, almost too opulent to operate. Then I stayed in a couple of roach motels, just to confirm my impression that too good was no better than really bad.

All this called for a poem, of course!

After a pretty good start I got this far, and this poem is still among my hundreds of unfinished.

Our Finest Hotel

As I hit the lavish lobby, I'm told at least
   twenty times,
"This is the city's finest!" (Oh boy, there
   go my dimes!)
"Our nicest suite," the bellboy says with
   stiff upper lip
I've been through this many times
   before, so I know what I'm about to
   grip.
In that room, behind those tall, brass-
   laden doors,
I can expect (in fact count on) some
   onerous opulence chores.
The bath towel will be too big to use,
   there'll be fourteen calls on hold.
The thermostat has two settings, cool
   and way too cold.
There'll be twenty lamps but little light—
   it'll be impossible to see.
and twenty calls and knocks, deluxe
   services designed to irritate poor me.
If you need to take a shower or bath, or
   perchance to wash your hair,
You'll need a booklet explaining how to
   use the overgrown hardware.
There'll be six pillows on the bed, and a
   tent-sized spread to move.
Before you sleep, I've heard it said,

And if you have a card for top execs, it's
   even worse, I'm told!
                              —DA September 1995

For one last example now, I'm a fanatic about being early. I believe it's the secret formula, the magic word for life and business success. One day on a gorgeous Seattle campus, I had a free morning. I'd had nine hours of sleep and the birds were singing, flowers blooming. I found a superb classical music station for my headphones and it was time for my master-piece on "early"—the poem of all poems! First I listed all the words that rhymed with "early": curly, burly, girlie, surely, pearly, whirly. Man, what a wimp choice! Then I programmed my little thesaurus to give me the synonyms for "early" and I got:

seasonably	prematurely	premature
soon	primitive	previous
timely	primordial	untimely

This didn't look too promising so I tried to hit it from a humorous angle—surely "early" is offers some great chances to poke fun. No help: the humor is there, but I couldn't seem to bring it forth. A moral slant is even more risky as most people are procrastinators who wouldn't want to take a beating in rhyme. So do I give up and rhyme "early" with "girlie" or chuck it and go have a bowl of oatmeal? I did the latter—a superior form of mush in this case.

Some poems are hard, they don't flow on your first, second, and even third attempt. Don't labor away at it until it becomes a hassle. Write the rough, take it as far as you can, and keep the ideas and progress you've made, no matter how bad. Then shelve the poem or file or post it for a while—a week, month, year, or five years. The changes in your maturity, vocabulary, and values over time may someday finish it for you with little or no effort.

The Silly, Sarcastic or Stupid: Don't Can It Too Quick

Poetry is a hand out from our heart that attempts to grab or hold something we felt deeply. Sometimes then later, in a different mood or at a different time or age, it may seem ridiculous. I've written a few lines in disgust, the heat of passion, or the urge for revenge, that I looked at the next day and said, "Gadfrey, I can't believe I wrote this!" It was too preachy or sweet or bitter, and so I tossed it.

I don't toss poems anymore, because if you felt an extreme of something, positive or negative, it has some value to remind, caution, or even discipline you in some way later when you re-read it and reflect. Just for kicks, keep your corn (for a while, anyway). The great Robert Browning of "How Do I Love Thee" fame in a moment of passionate sorrow, buried one of his poems with his wife. Later when he got to thinking about it or desperate for a sale, her dug her up to get the poem back.

Just keep those poems that are clearly "for your eyes only" at this point in one of your less accessible files!

Don't Worry About the "Duds"

Sure you'll be enthusiastic about many subjects and write lots of poems—maybe piles of them. And you'll be the first to admit, reading them objectively later, that some of them miss the mark pretty far. It's important to produce a few "duds." Some-times they won't work—you'll have to write a lot to come up with a jewel or two. It's like making pottery—even a fine artist standing by his premium prize winner could tell you about the other thirty at home, on the bench or shelf, that didn't come out as well as this one (even though they felt good in his hand at the time). If it takes two dozen poems to produce one prize one, get to work on the two dozen now!

CHAPTER EIGHT

What to do with your poems

You'll be amazed how fast your poems will accumulate (years go by quickly!). You'll have stacks, piles, and then drawers and boxes of them, and often when the big moment comes to use one, you'll rummage like a crazed junk collector trying to put your hands on it.

For years I had my poems all over—jammed into drawers and notebooks and files, and they became mixed and scattered. Every time I needed one, it was rummage and dig and unwrinkle. Finally I put my poems all together in a big binder. Then it got to bulging, and letting some fine tidbits slip away.

I don't have a general file anymore!

Today, I have much better filing or "keep track of" system for my poetry. I make extra copies of all my poems as mentioned earlier, and keep copies of them in different places (in case of fire or loaning loss). The originals are now put in separate files or binders with labels like:

Poems in Progress (the ones I am working on now—I carry these with me)

"In-house" Poems (verses for family, friends, neighbors, business associates, special occasions, and personal remembrances)

Poems of Opinion, or "I'm going to change the world" verses

Short Self-Helps

Longer Self-Helps

Love and Romance

Rhyme for Music

Other Poems

Poems I Admire

Poems from Friends

Good Poem Ideas for Someday

Failures and Fizzles (incomplete, unsatisfying poems)

The topics or categories of your own poems will be a lot different, of course. When a write a new poem, I always make multiple copies. Then I pass or send some around as needed, and bring the originals home and just slide them into the appropriate notebook or binder, later punching holes in the pages and officially mounting them.

Poems by others that I see or hear and like, I buy in books or photocopy from the source, make extras, pass them around, and put a copy in my "Poems I Admire" file.

Short vs. Long "Self-Helps"

In case you're wondering what those categories of mine meant: Many people who want help, self-help from reading or listening, want it fast. They don't want a whole book or long essay or epistle to pore over, in hopes of finding a fragment or two of brilliance. Short self-helps would be one or two lines like:

An apple a day keeps the doctor away.

It's the set of the sail, and not the gale,
That decides the way you go.

A long self-help is a poem that has a story of some sort, develops a moral that you have to wait to the end to grasp—like a gunfighter ballad, for instance.

When I looked at the height of the stack of poems in each of my categories, I was interested to see that the "In-house poems," poems of personal remembrance or for special occasions (the kind we all have occasion to write every week) totaled more than all of the others combined. I always thought I was one of the original romance poets and was amazed to see I had only a few in my "Love and Romance" file.

When You Finish a Verse

When you get a verse finished, write or type a final copy, date it (as to when it was written), and put your name on it.

When you start patching and revising your poem a bit, you can easily lose track of which "edition" it is. So mark it clearly at the top, in the corner, or somewhere: "First rough," "Second draft," "Final," etc.

Then, as mentioned earlier, be SURE to make several copies of the poem.

Prettier in Print!

All of us picture (and are used to reading) poetry as printed, not handwritten. Nothing is tougher than reading poetry in longhand—even when it's your own poetry and your own writing! Much poetry may be written first in longhand but it isn't wise to leave it or pass it around in that form. Not only is handwriting, especially other people's, hard to read, but poetry needs an unbroken flow and rhythm, whether read aloud or in silence, to yourself. When it's handwritten, you'll stumble along trying to determine whether it's an "i" or an "e", some people make "n's" and "r's" the same, etc. Once your poetry is printed, via typewriter or computer, it really looks like a poem. The words are plain and easily read, and the message can come out and the rhyme happen. With a handwritten poem, on the other hand, readers will be concentrating more on translation than on the poem's tribute.

Another value of printing or typing is that it makes the length of the lines and stanzas clearer. This makes editing easier, to get the right metrical emphasis and balance.

Plus typed words just plain look more appealing than cramped, uneven handwriting. And your poem will fit on one page instead of three!

DARE TO SHARE
Your Poetry!

You'll either hide, carry around, or shyly read your first poems to someone. With any success or encouragement you'll produce more. Rather magically over the years you'll accumulate a bunch of poems (and you'll save all of them, even the two-liners).

Now what? Is there a "dare to share" spirit in you, an urge to flaunt, even?

Poems and photographs have something in common—they need (pardon the pun) to be exposed. They have to move or affect someone, something, somehow, sometime, or what good are they, really? They need to be an active, not passive entity in life.

Or to put it another way, in verse, of course:

> You write well! (Now some sighs)
> Why, this is worthy of others' eyes!
> Let's get it cleaned up. Why let it croak?
> And share it with all of those other folk.

Let's look at poetry's big three:

PERCEIVE
(the thought that inspires)

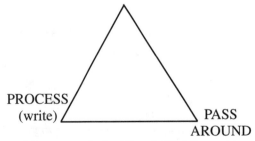

PROCESS
(write)   PASS
                            AROUND

Many people do #1 and #2. All want to do #3 but few do. Number three is simply presenting our work to the public, publishing it or passing it around.

Once you have your poems typed up, and have made at least three or four copies of them, then you can:

1. Pass one (or many) of them around.

2. Read them to family and friends. Once you start watching for them, you will find more occasions than you imagined to read and share your poems.

3. Post your poems wherever their feeling and message might be appreciated.

4. Use them in classes or those many times we are called upon to give personal wisdom or advice.

5. You can even have your verse superimposed on a photograph or doily, or printed up and laminated to a placque or mounted in a frame for gifts. Loosen up, be creative. I'm not a fan of lettered T-shirts but I must admit to seeing a few with clever verses silk-screened on them that got some "oohs" and "ahhs" out of me! For some of these special purposes you might consider rendering your poetry in clear and beautiful (or at least very neat) handwriting.

You can go overboard when it comes to circulating your poetry, so be careful. It's OK to make a dozen copies and pass them to family and friends, or to do up maybe fifty or even a hundred or so for a company get-together or family reunion. Just remember that poems are often like "good jokes"—only good when they fit the occasion. Our goal is to **affect** people with our poetry, not inflict it on them!

When reading or quoting from one your poems during a talk or speech, don't announce, "I have a little poem here for you." Or page through a notebook or book in front of them to find it. You don't need to identify poems or jokes ahead to justify them. Don't let the audience know what is coming, just launch right into it cold turkey and they will flow into it right along with you.

HOW ABOUT A WHOLE BOOK OF YOUR OWN POETRY?

The simplest way to do this is to bind the poems you would like to share with others into one booklet. You can have copies of your poems made whatever size you like, and then staple, saddle stitch, or put them together in a comb binding. Any of these can be done quickly, easily, and inexpensively.

Bind at least three copies:
1. One to keep somewhere.
2. One to carry with you.
3. One to pass around or lend out.

It's nice to have everything together in a secure, compact package, like having your eggs in one basket instead of all different pockets! It's much easier and more pleasant to read bound pages than loose sheets. Your poems will be easier to review, add to, and share.

THE NEXT STEP: PUBLISHING YOUR OWN POEMS

You can class up your collection even more by publishing it yourself, as a book of poems that are all yours. Publishing an entire book of your own poetry is much easier than it used to be—we've got it made when it comes to this, compared to the days of Longfellow, Milton, and Keats. The means available to record and circulate our poems are almost endless, and much less expensive and easier to come by than ever before. Computers with laser printers, hundreds of type styles to choose from, plus all kinds of borders and outlines and clip art, even color! We should take advantage of all this. Have you ever noticed what a good frame can do for an average picture?

These days, anyone with a computer can be a desktop publisher. If you don't have a computer, there are people everywhere who do, and can input and lay out every page of your book attractively.

Putting together a book of poems is easy to do. Just round up the poems you want to share, and put them in a nice, readable order—organize them by some logic or order of presentation.

Choose a clear, readable type style that you like, or creates the effect you have in mind, and lay the poems out attractively, preferably one poem per page.

The layout and decoration of your finished poem on the page is about as exciting as the poem-writing process itself. Check out and consider borders, decorative lines, or small bits of art that might enhance your verse. Just be careful not to let the frosting smother the cake here.

Print out a clean black and white copy of your book for an original to take to the printer or copy shop. If you need to keep your production costs reasonable, illustrations should be black and white as well. Illustrations with clean lines will reproduce best.

Choose a heavier paper for the cover of your book, and pick a good title and set it off in large type on the cover.

Be sure to include a copyright line at the front of the book, "© Copyright 1999 by _____" [your name or the name you want to copyright the book in].

If you don't have a computer and laser printer, take your collection to Kinko's or other copy shop and they will give you a bid on doing all the work for you. They will also copy and bind just the number of books you wish (if your Christmas shopping list has 17 family and friends, there's no reason to print 100 books).

Local print shops can also produce small books, as can any of the "short run" printers who are geared to producing books in small quantities. Just to give you an idea here: 50 to 200 books will probably cost $3-$5 each; 1,000-3,000 books about $2.50 to $3.00 a book, depending of course on the size of the book and the number of pages. If you print 5,000 books the price goes down to $1.00 to $2.00 a book.

Once you have a book in your hands you can pass your poems around in first-class form, even sell them.

Just remember, poetry is a tough sell. People love their own, but they're not always as enthusiastic about the efforts of others. Don't be too disappointed if and when people don't ask for more copies or a hardcover edition.

(Are those poems good enough to enter into a contest, or maybe even sell to a publisher?....)

BEING PUBLISHED

No matter how much our poetry benefits us writing it, for some strange reason many people feel none of this really counts unless their poems (or even one poem) is published. Even if you don't get paid for that publication—and generally you won't—suddenly wearing the label of "the published poet among us" is heap big medicine in the writing world.

Talk about motivation plus to write! Getting pleasure from poems is enough, winning a contest is wonderful, but seeing your poem in print and maybe even getting paid for it too sounds like just short of Heaven for us and our verse.

It does feel good to have the acknowledgment of seeing your work of any kind (art, song, essay, poem) used by someone else. Don't let yourself get hung up on this, however. I know published poets and other writers whose best stuff isn't as good as your worst, so don't fret too much. Enjoy what you write for your own use and pleasure, and I'll promise you that some of your "pass-around" poems (ones that are passed around within the family or your business or company) will be read and appreciated more than some of the published ones.

If you are really serious about publication, pick up a copy of a nice fat volume called *Poet's Market*. It has more than a thousand places to seek a wider audience for your poems, and all kinds of helpful how-to advice besides. It covers everything and is well worth checking out at the library, or investing in your very own copy of. You can get it at bookstores, or by calling or writing to F & W Publications, 1507 Dana Avenue, Cincinnati, OH 45207. 1-800-289-0963.

Writer's Digest Magazine, too, has lots of contest opportunities for poets and some excellent articles on the art of poetry as well.

The following lines by an aspiring poet like you do a good job of expressing some of the pitfalls of the path to publication:

A Hard Dollar

The grind starts
after the last dot and title are in
* place.*
The taste of glue on stamps and
* envelopes*
the roulette of submission and
* rejection*
and the long waits for a sale
wear patience to rubble
Poetry is a hard dollar.

A dab of the work and a little of
* the fun*
come in finding a reader
who can see yes instead of va-
* cancy*
connections instead of mist
allusions instead of non sequitors
and us as worthy instead of idiots.
*   —Grace Longeneker*

Is it a Sin to Sell Your Poetry?

For years I loved reading the short lines of the poet named Richard Armour. I never met him, knew nothing about him, only that his verse was good and rich. Reading even one of his four-liners, you grinned and nodded and learned. Mr. Armour's poetry appeared in many maga- zines and it was high grade ore—wonder- ful.

One day on one of these publications' editorial page some "poets" wrote in and criticized Mr. Armour for making money with his poetry. They didn't feel he was a real poet because his work was light and cash worthy.

That really got to me. Those dry critics couldn't raise an eyebrow with their lifetime of work, let alone a cent to pay for it. What is more worthy than selling your work? Why is poetry any different from the art of a carpenter or a mason, it builds, too, so why isn't it worth money? More power to Richard Armour and others like him. Any mileage or money you get out of a good poem isn't disgraceful, it is rewarding and an indication that someone wants and likes it and is willing to pay for it. I say, "Wow!" Mr. Armour, you sure brought lots of goodness into my life and I'm sure many others'.

A Word About Others' Opinions and Comments on Your Verse

One of our biggest fears, and surely the biggest reason many of us won't put out the poetry of our heart, is anticipation of "what others will say or think about it." Poems are pretty personal when you get down to it—people can criticize our car or our dog, our yard, state, country and even our singing voice or dress code and most of us can live with that. But poems, now that is getting close to our inner being and can really get to us. (That goes both ways, of course—whether others are praising our poetry or pooh-poohing it.)

You write something really good about an event at the company meeting, for example, and one of the supervisors who happens to like verse tells you, "Hey, Morgan, that was pretty good, you ought to type that up and copy off a few and hand them out at the closing event of the confer- ence." You are absolutely elated, this is like being short-range published! So you labor over that poem and polish it, type it up, run off two hundred copies on some nice beige paper, and do pass them out to all two hundred of your employees and their families at the meeting.

After the closing ceremonies everyone is gone, but your poems aren't. They took the menus, note pads, the matches, and the awful hotel mints, but there right out in front of most places on the tables lies your wonderful verse. Some copies have water marks from being used as napkins or coasters, others are doodled on, several made into airplanes, even your spouse left hers sitting there, talk about rejection in print!

What do you do about this? Give the perceptive supervisor who recognized your genius a promotion to CEO and fire the rest and divorce your mate? That might be the emotion that floods over you, but remember, even the all-time masters have their stuff tread on by the unappreciative public. Let it go and keep writing. Several people did read your poem and take it home and read it to others and some made copies of it and spread it around the office. And of course you inspired and showed the way for the other young or timid would-be writers—showed them how and what to do. And your verses may have touched the minds and affected the lives of many, even if the majority of those photocopies were left on the table… you did right!

There is an unprecedented jealousy among writers and poets like I've seen nowhere else. They may be too polite to come out with it openly but they (the writing world) often boils inside with envy about others' success on the page… so roll with it and keep writing. Even if you read one of your verses and someone leaves the room or grimaces… continue! Really who is the poet critic of the world? I know there are plenty of intellectuals who think they are eminently qualified to judge good and bad when it comes to poetry, but are they even as qualified as a fourth-grade class who stares in fascination or roars in laughter over a verse being read by the teacher, anyone's verse… maybe yours? Remember you are writing poetry first for **yourself**, if you like it… it's good!

Don't Constantly Compare Yourself to Others

Our constant comparison of "ours" with "theirs" is a big wet blanket in life. I'll bet we could cure this hangup in a hurry if we just once could see all of the "top" poet's drafts, rejects, and failures. We live them so we do see our own shortcomings, but we seldom see others' shortfalls, so their show seems perfect right out of the chute.

I remember when my company first contracted to clean in Las Vegas one of the clients insisted we see a spectacular Vegas show and bought us tickets. From an audience view it was spectacular—the light and sound effects, fireworks and "anatomy" were astonishing, breath catching. The dazzling routines, colorful clothing, and lack of it certainly made their point.

For months the visual and mental impact of that show stuck with me. Then we were invited by that very hotel to bid on their maintenance service. They took us through the whole building, every part. And there backstage, were the props and outfits we'd seen on stage, and now we were seeing them up close—no fanfare, just hanging on pegs, frayed and faded, sweat stained, patched, and soiled. I gasped and thought "Boy, what I have at home is sure higher grade, lovelier than this." Your own is of value just by being **yours**.

And then there are those of us who won't do something because someone else can do it better. That's like us not eating because "they" aren't hungry. The purpose of poetry, and for that matter most things is not competition—we seem to get carried away with comparisons and measurements and ratings Sure some pocketknives and watches are "better," but all cut or tell time regardless of their guts or glitter. When it comes to poetry I'd place "fit" above "fine" any day. Your thoughts are your thoughts, your heart is your heart, and you aren't (shouldn't be) writing poems for a contest, you are doing it for yourself, and maybe those closest to you.

No one feels, sees, senses just like you, you are unique—that makes your product special. Fifth place in a country fair pie contest doesn't mean your pie isn't delicious, nourishing, and satisfying. So bake that poem or lots of them!!!

Just Compare Yourself to Yourself!

There are kindergarten poems by kindergarten kids that are absolutely great, and fourth and sixth grade poems that are brilliant for that age and level of comprehension. However when you are a senior in college or a mature forty-eight with your first grandchild, there should be a maturing of the quality of your poems. They should have a little deeper thought, and little better meter, more impact, get their points across more concisely, and so on. Just compare yourself to yourself!

Watch Those Criticisms of Others, too

Is there good and bad poetry?

That's like asking if there is an ugly baby. Beauty is in the promise of edification, so even bad poetry (misspelled, poorly structured stuff) can have value.

Most want-to-be writers of verse are infatuated with their first few lines, they really treasure those first efforts, no matter how crude. So if you edit or suggest alterations to people's "first" you are calling their beloved baby ugly. Our first is our finest, right? (Mostly because it is often our "only.") I've learned to be carefuller than careful when it comes to giving an opinion on a beginner's work. Honesty is not always the best policy here.

I rationalize any highly subjective, strained, or exaggerated compliments I may utter by telling myself if the poem can enlighten, moderate, or sensitize someone—or get a smile from them—it surely has as much value as some of the pro stuff that's got a million groans from classrooms over the years.

If You Like It, Grab It!

One way to raise your appreciation of poetry and help learn how to do your own is be sure to get a copy of any poem you really like. Someone in a speech or sermon, class or lecture, or any situation, will come up with a quote or poem that really hits home or supports their point. If you and everyone else really likes it, look around—not one (maybe one) in the entire audience or room will write the name of it or a few words of it down.

I always go to the speaker afterward and ask, "Where did you get that?" If I love the poem, I ask what its title is and who wrote it. Half of the time, they will hand you a copy. Poetry lovers love to share. Others will tell you the name and you can look it up. I was at business luncheon once and the speaker came forth with the following poem (it just fit the subject of being prepared, which he was speaking on):

I ran up to him afterwards and asked who wrote it. " I did." he said and I had a copy in my hands in no time.

Clip, copy down, or buy a copy of what you like, what touches you, NOW. Get it, grab it, glean it, now. Nothing is more frustrating than trying to locate a line you loved...later! By the way where is the following from: "the wheel will never turn again with water that is past"... ? If you know, call me!

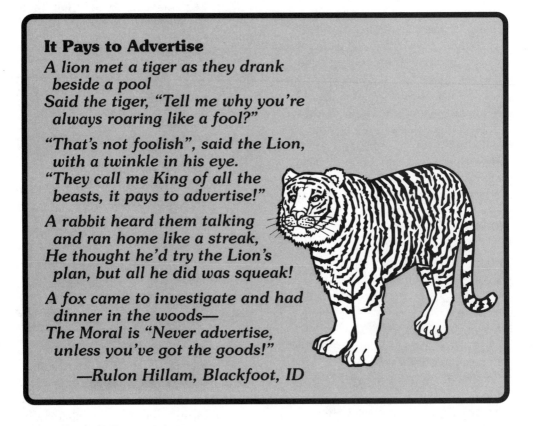

It Pays to Advertise

A lion met a tiger as they drank
  beside a pool
Said the tiger, "Tell me why you're
  always roaring like a fool?"

"That's not foolish", said the Lion,
  with a twinkle in his eye.
"They call me King of all the
  beasts, it pays to advertise!"

A rabbit heard them talking
  and ran home like a streak,
He thought he'd try the Lion's
  plan, but all he did was squeak!

A fox came to investigate and had
  dinner in the woods—
The Moral is "Never advertise,
  unless you've got the goods!"

—Rulon Hillam, Blackfoot, ID

What makes a good poem

- Collecting notes and ideas before
- Making sure it has purpose and direction
- Thinking of several different angles on the subject, and then narrowing it to the best
- Keeping it short as possible while still delivering the message
- Writing it WHEN you feel it
- Redoing your rough a couple of times
- Reading it out loud to yourself
- Making sure it isn't too predictable
- Giving it a good title
- Typing it up
- Having several copies of it
- Laying it out handsomely

What makes a weak poem

- Failing to pick up the pencil
- Giving up when you can't find a rhyme
- Getting hung up on the "rules and regulations" of poetry
- Accepting your first draft when you don't even like it
- Rambling and repeating yourself after the point is made
- Moralizing and preaching
- Aiming for "poetic and profound" rather than clear and enjoyable
- Jerky rhyme
- Bad taste and crudeness
- Keeping it in handwriting
- Listening to too many opinions on it
- Keeping it hidden forever in a drawer

One last thought now:
Don't Let the "Ben's Father's" of the World Get to You

Reading Ben Franklin's autobiography, I really disliked his father. Ben Franklin was a man of much wit and wisdom and highly influential in the development of our great country, both politically and economically. He worked in his dad's print shop as a young person and got pretty good at not just proofreading, but English and grammar and the use of them, too. One of their customers, an ingenious fellow with a good-sized library of his own, took a liking to Ben and invited him to browse his many books. He even lent some to Franklin, who said, "I now took a fancy to poetry and made some little pieces." His brother loved them and encouraged Ben to write more. He wrote about recent events, printed up his poems, and they sold well. Ben was motivated, "but my father discouraged me by ridiculing my performances and telling me verse-makers were generally beggars. So I escaped being a poet."

Bad dad, I'd say. With all that Ben Franklin was capable of and knowing he liked poetry, think of the collections we would have today if he hadn't been belittled by his father's criticisms. Don't let the "Ben's fathers" of this world get to you. Some of your rhyme might be Hefty bag fodder at first, but then even the greatest poets have seen more recycling of their parchment (or bond) than they would care to admit. Don't let it bother you for a minute, just keep on writing and Go for it!

Places and ways to use verse

Poems have a place anyplace, and it really is a shame how much masterful poetry is and has been on the shelf, in a drawer or a closed book for who knows how long. Poetry needs to be out there working—serving some use, giving some satisfaction, not stashed and hidden away.

Consider all the life situations where poetry can express or communicate: Love, joy, pleasure, puzzlement, leaving, arriving, anger, annoyance, sorrow, happiness, amazement, the weather, natural scenes, journeys, thoughts, dreams, events, chil-

dren, marriage, divorce, quitting, beginning or ending something, sickness, passion, instructions, warnings, complaints, congratulations, insults, death, bereavement, promises, thanks, hello, good-bye, spiritual or religious thoughts or musings.

Name one of these life situations where poetry will take a second place for expression or communication.

You have the situations and events in your life, all you have to do is remember to put poetry to use in them.

Think of poetry's power to:
get attention
get a laugh
release tension
blaze a path
cause a sigh
sing a song
teach a moral
right a wrong
heal a quarrel
change a flow
show a knack
cause a know
fill a lack
brace a spine
cause a bond
build a mind
cross a pond

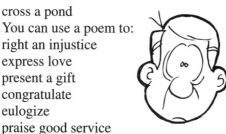

You can use a poem to:
right an injustice
express love
present a gift
congratulate
eulogize
praise good service
report bad service
record a trip
remember a trial
give an award
soften a disappointment
celebrate a success
point out something funny
thank someone
praise someone
   recognize accomplishment
   express frustration or anger
express faith or record a spiritual
   experience
   inspire

Anything and everything
can be done better in poetry!

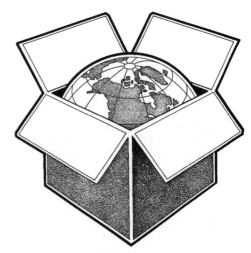

Poems don't have to be earthshaking to shake the earthling!

Aren't there times in life when… "Boy, this is great!", "I love you," or "Oh, thank you very much!" just don't cut it? You might sincerely feel it, mean it, and say it, but it still doesn't seem enough, it feels weak and watered down and ordinary. Well it is time for verse to come to the rescue, and your verse, no matter how inexperienced or experienced a poet you may be, still carries more impact than the cold, professionally printed verse inside the Mother's Day cards, get-well cards, and valentines. Say it yourself!

Why let some "professional" write a mass-produced poem for you when they don't even know your mom, sweetheart, boss, or the sickness at hand? Think about it, you are better qualified, you have the same tools at your command as the pro, and for sure a better instinct and feeling for the occasion.

The following little "encyclopedia of poemcrafting" is meant to help and encourage you to put poetry to use in the endless opportunities that present themselves to us......every week, day, and year.

GUIDE TO POEM TYPES

FAMILY POETRY

The poems done within groups and especially families are some of the best and most touching verses around. They generally get passed around (these days, that means across the country) and read and reread by the whole family.

I have a whole wall of small file drawers in my home office and I keep a drawer for each of my children and grandchildren and tuck little morsels and messages in there as they come along. One night my wife and I came home after Cindy, our youngest daughter, but before our next daughter, Elizabeth, who wasn't by any means the least popular girl in high school. This note from Cindy (age fourteen) was pinned to Liz's pillow.

It was not only a laugh and a nice way to deliver some instructions, but a real compliment and bond of care, from a sister looking out for her sister. Best of all, it was spontaneous! For something like this poetry cannot be equaled.

All our children had their enthusiasms and projects, but Liz wrote (and inspired) the most poetry. When she was six her goodness and kindness to others was unmatched. Watching her help out one evening, I jotted this down and tossed it into her file. That was twenty-five years ago. Today it brings back the vision and the appreciation of having good children.

DEAR LIZ

HOPE your date was Lots of Fun
   Now could you ever be a Nun?
With boys to take you every where
   You can go through Life Without a Care.
Now before you Turn in for the Night
   Please Turn out every Shiny light.
The Shiny TREE With Presents Round
   The plug it is upon the Ground
The Shiny Star up in the Sky
   Please turn it of and don't Ask why.
The Nativity Set Sitting Peacefully
   Pull the Plug and don't Wake me.
Now that you have done this Chore,
   And are sure there are no more.
Off to bed you now must Go
   'A Mid-night SNACK? NO, NO, NO!
So Goodnight I'll say to you
   & AND don't Forget your Scriptures too.
                Love
                Little
                Sis
                Cin

82

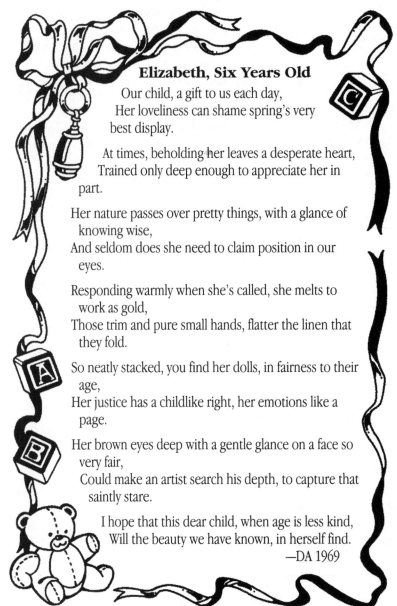

Elizabeth, Six Years Old

Our child, a gift to us each day,
Her loveliness can shame spring's very
best display.

At times, beholding her leaves a desperate heart,
Trained only deep enough to appreciate her in
part.

Her nature passes over pretty things, with a glance of
knowing wise,
And seldom does she need to claim position in our
eyes.

Responding warmly when she's called, she melts to
work as gold,
Those trim and pure small hands, flatter the linen that
they fold.

So neatly stacked, you find her dolls, in fairness to their
age,
Her justice has a childlike right, her emotions like a
page.

Her brown eyes deep with a gentle glance on a face so
very fair,
Could make an artist search his depth, to capture that
saintly stare.

I hope that this dear child, when age is less kind,
Will the beauty we have known, in herself find.
—DA 1969

My mother-in-law, Grandma Vera, was one of the choice individuals who have ever lived on this earth. She made peace and brought family and good feelings together wherever she went. She was so appreciative of any praise or attention. When I'd write a verse about her, she would beam and show it around and copy it and read and reread it. So I always used verse to thank her and make her feel good.

One day she and her husband Jerry had a bargaining session over a battered old rocking chair which Grandma tried to sneak into the moving van that was moving their earthly possessions to their retirement home in Arizona. I did a poem on the event that brought lots of laughs to both the family and friends:

Grandma Vera's Rocking Chair

At Christmas in the grandkids' house
Grandma got some gifts.
A teddy bear was one...
and a package too big to lift!

Granny tore the paper away
While Jerry gave an icy stare
Would it fit in the travel trailer?
Ye gads! A portable rocking chair!

Grandma fondled it kindly
While Jerry said with a sneer,
"That thing is too big to take along,
you'll have to leave it here."

Grandma bawled and cried big tears
Even confessed to smuggling the Alaska
   ladder.
And promised to leave 600 pounds of pills
   behind
If she could take along that fold up "satter."

Grandpa finally consented
And said, "I know it's wrong.
But you can wrap it in a blanket
And take that worthless thing along."

And so in went Grandma's rocking chair
To some warm climate south.
"Toothpick fodder?" Grandpa Jerry eyed it.
Grandma kept a tight closed mouth.

Grandma could just see herself,
Rocking in the sun.
Her own special custom chair
Why, she'd be the only one.

But, ha, the tables turned.
Her bottom was never planted.
Cause Jerry claimed squatter's rights
And its possession he was granted.

He just sat in it to tie his shoe
Boy, it sure fit well.
When Grandma tried to claim her gift
Jerry told her to go to ....(the couch inside).

Jerry teetered to and fro
And became addicted to that throne.
He wouldn't even leave his place
For a steaming hot T-bone.

"Charlie's Angel's" or shuffleboard,
Could not wrench Jerry loose.
As he relaxed and read in that fine chair,
Contented as a goose.

Jerry loved that chair so much
He relaxed too much to talk.
When models in bikinis strolled in front of
   him,
he never missed a rock.

Ol' Grandma had no place to sit
Except upon the ground.
Cause Jerry hourly rocked away,
With a squeaky, creaky sound.

Grandma's now back in Idaho all alone
While Jerry just rocks away.
Reading, lounging in the southern sun
Now you can't beat that, I'd say.
          —DA 1980

I don't want to engulf you in the family album here, but I do want to ask you to think about some "family" ideas for poetry—for your own family, or even other families. Family poems for example can be good-byes, welcome homes, or "I miss you" poems. Our third daughter and her husband once went to Hong Kong for a business conference. As no one is a good enough babysitter to watch four little ones between one and nine years old, my wife and I took the grandparent assignment at their home. It didn't take those kids long to miss their parents and they began planning a special homecoming.

"Grandpa help us!" They liked to sing and act so I used some simple verse in the "bong-bong" rhythm of an oriental gong. When the parents did return home and stepped through the door, the kids lined up, dressed to play the part (complete with fans and chopsticks) as they sang in broken English:

You stay too long-ong in
 Hong Kong
Lots and lots happen
 while you gone!

Jason dumped his mush
 on Grandpa's chair,
Little budda Christopher, ate
 cupboard bare.

We make plentee noise, we have much
 much fun
Grandma-San so shakee, she no can dial
 911.

You stay too long-ong in Hong Kong
We teach Emily nursery rhymes all wrong.

We order greasy pizza almost every night
And every night by bedtime, this place a
 messy sight!

We glad you home so fast we clean the rugs,
in trade for plenty presents, and great big
 hugs.

Their parents even videoed this and it was a delight to all the lives involved. Verse can welcome so well.

Encouraging Young People to Write Poetry

Don't overestimate the age requirements of the "poetry club" or "poet's circle." Take every opportunity to encourage and help children with simple rhyme. They love it and can and will come up with the darndest, most delightful bits of rhyme. Poetry will be a super way for them to communicate with and catch the attention of their peers, and provide high-class enjoyment for themselves and others.

It will also build confidence and cultivate sensitivity. The impact of childhood experiences is never equaled again in our lives. Only then are we open and fresh and appreciative and objective enough to absorb the purity of things. Encourage young people to record those lifetime impressions. Write their verses down for them if you need to, post them, and praise them.

Here are some examples of "wee poetry" I've picked up:

A house a hourse
Of corc ofcorc thats
all I ever wot, a hourse

I love this, and found it after some little first grader had gone to bed, in their pile of notes and scribbles. A testimony of a child's heart's desire in poetry. I think for the author's age this is master-equal.

One of my grandchildren was asked by her teacher to write a poem about a favorite place, to the rhythm of some familiar tune. She wrote the following to the tune of "Home, Home, on the Range." Wayne county (and Capitol Reef National Park), the subject of her poem, is in deep southern Utah.

Home, Home, in Wayne

Oh let me go, to a place we all know,
That has lots of places to go.
It's a hiker's delight
When the birds take flight
And they see all the beauty of Wayne.

Home, Home in Wayne.
Where farmers and planters grow grain.
There are mountains and lakes,
and rattlesnakes.
And the roads are not crouded all day.
—Amy Simons

For a Thanksgiving holiday program at the high school, my daughter Liz and a couple of friends wrote a poem that involved a good fairy appearing and granting a couple of the students a wish. Their wish was that the principal, Mr. Jolley, become whatever he said to the students. It got exciting when entire school beheld the 180-pound principal turned into a Thanksgiving turkey:

It was such a surprise
that Mr. Jolley was
perky
As he watched their behavior and
said, "Well, I'll be the turkey."
ZAP, the fairy came through and
there in his tie
stood our leader… a turkey
seven feet high!

The poem this stanza came from did its job, it worked! It got the attention of the class, enlivened a dull day at school, and gave the principal a chuckle.

Like you, I'm a keeper. I save pictures, notes, sayings, letters, and poems that impress or depress me.

As I mentioned earlier, I taught literature in high school for a couple of years, many years ago. While working on this book I went back and looked for any poem from the students and "lo" I had kept some! Look at some of these lines that fifteen to seventeen year olds wrote overnight. It did them an enormous amount of good and all of them were really proud of their work.

Life has many hardships,
But the hardest one to bear,
Is when life is ending,
And no one seems to care.
—Mr. BB

I am but a man
Yet I see
I am but a man
Yet I love
No bounds of black
Restrain my immortality.
—Miss JP

In an old, back alley street,
Where the gang delights to meet,
The place of planning good and bad,
Without regard for Mom and Dad.
The fate of this great nation
Is being decided from these low stations.
—J. H.

Some of our family lives in Skagway, Alaska. That is way, way up in North among the glaciers. It's a small town, but full of big-hearted family and friends. Our teenage granddaughter, Mindy, is a beautiful young woman who runs an ice cream store, clothing store, and video store. She participates in track, is a paramedic and a cheerleader and star basketball player—a real go-getter. In the rush of all these activities—work and home and school and growing up—there is also a serious side to Mindy. The sacred space deep inside us that governs the outer space of conduct. We stayed in Skagway a couple of weeks one summer and helped Mindy's parents paint and clean and pick blueberries on the Alaska slopes. Cleaning one room to paint it, I found this on the floor behind a dresser, apparently some verse Mindy had scribbled out when she was fourteen or fifteen. I was impressed with it and she said I could have it.

One day I'll just go and play, forget the job,
the rough road ahead.
I'll set myself free and smell the sweet
fragrance of roses beneath me.
One day I'll just cry, maybe for no reason,
but when I do that one day,
I'll cry rivers of tears washing pain, removing vain.
One day, I'll listen to make up for time
forgotten, to hear happy tunes or one of
nature's glories.
One day, I'll die and yes, most of us know
why.
He is sad for some, joyous for others but
one thing I'll remember is, I'll see my
Heavenly Father.

Capturing thoughts in poems or essays like this is a critical part of growing up and will mean a lot for remembrance some day. We keep on growing all our lives—we are growing at age 30, 40, 50, 60, 70, and 80!! Do capture it!

Poetry for Reunions

Reunions!!! Now here is a place even the novice of all novices can get a good start writing verse. No matter how good or bad, boring or banal the lines here may be, if they are full of family names and situations, family history and events, the poem is good.

The carpenter that built in our community for years, Leo Bullock, is a prime example. The old gentleman was the least likely poet, it might have appeared, of any person around. Yet at the Bullock family reunion, he pulled out a two-pager tracing each of the eleven Bullock boys' births and life. It was great with lines like:

But Mabel felt much different, in those hot
July winds.
Then when it happened, I'll be damned, it
was twins.
But by the time that I was three I heard my
father tell
I couldn't have come from heaven, cause I
was too full of Hell.

The family loved it and I asked for a copy for my file and after reading it, I appreciated the Bullock boys of the community even more.

In writing reunion or other family poems, remember that the more family members you can manage to include in your verse, the kinder your audience will be. Small, isolated events, no matter how rich or memorable, won't give many a chance to hear "their name."

Be sure to make plenty of copies, too.

Saying THANK-YOU Better

Well... I think it is better and maybe I'll convince you to try it, if you haven't already.

One thing we'd all like to be better at is being thankful and appreciative—when we express our thanks to a benefactor or donor it often seems to fall short of what we really feel. The words "thank you," "thanks," "thanks a lot" or even "thank you very much" just don't transfer the feeling we intended. Thank-you cards, too, don't really carry the clout or appreciation we feel. Even a quickly composed or hand-written poem carries a good message here. It says you've given more than money, or just a word or two and a signature. A personally versed thank-you beats a pre-printed message on a commercial card (and saves the up to $5.00 it now costs for a card you don't fully like). Guess which "thank-you" the receiver will show around the most, keep the longest, and remember best?

Remember each thank-you is one hundred percent yours, so no one can infringe on it or make judgments about it. It is **your** thank-you, so mushy or master-ful, it doesn't matter, it's all up to you. The intent and thought is what matters and it will do a lot for the recipient.

So leave convention, routine, and ordinary habits behind and tailor your thank-you to your true and inner, maybe one of a kind reasons for thanking the person. When a family member was in the hospital once, my former "right hand" (and still part-time) employee brought a wonderful homemade tray of food. I sent the pan back with:

Ode to Nancy's Rolls

To the rescue, many times
Those fresh baked biscuits
  came.
Nourishment, warm and good,
Deserving cooking fame.

But best of all, they delivered us
From Pocatello Regional bacteria,
Those rolls and jam saved us indeed,
From the hospital cafeteria.
                    —DA April 1996

Another time, a friend of mine sent the best box of homemade jam and jelly from his farm. As you know, treats like these aren't an assembly-line product. It is time consuming, picking those tiny berries, then de-bugging and de-stemming them and boiling and bottling. A single jar of anything in this line of home food products, if time is weighed at all, is a real gift. This man was a literary agent and was good at his canning, as me and everyone at our family table witnessed. So I put a few minutes extra into my thank-you:

Ode to Oscar's Syrup

A miracle of faith and toil
To grow them in Ohio soil.
But yield those bushes, the berries black,
And currants besides in Oscar's sack.
Boiling and squeezing and measuring, too,
Created he that master's brew
Of perfect syrup, jarred no less,
That Aslett's table came to bless.
On fresh, full-flavored wheat pancakes,
Twas most elite for hunger aches.
An agent, maybe, good with geese,
We vote Oscar—"syrup expertise!"
—the poet who savored the super syrup

88

> You can say the words or write notes or send gifts, but giving someone a special verse, written just for them, as a thank-you… is a just plain nice—in fact wonderful—way to use your own poems.

Be creative with CONGRATULATIONS!

People are bored with the same old ways of saying "congratulations"—placcques, trophies, certificates, and the like. A poem would be much more memorable and appreciated at those times of: promotion, birth, marriage, and so on. A poem is small, and easy to keep and display. Above all it's personal, much more personal than an engraved pen or even a gold watch. Even a very short verse can do this. Such as:

Great job, Hank
now head of the bank!

or for a group:

We were going to call you on the
  phone
But now that you've entered the
  presidential zone
We'll congratulate you with a different tone
And rush right in to get a loan!
  —The gang on the lower floor

PAT ON THE BACK VERSE

Poetry works equally well when it comes to commending someone for an accomplishment or a job well done.

A poem is much better than an ordinary acknowledgment or thank-you

because it says by its very existence that you really DO care. Poor or non-recognition of a good deed can be close to back stabbing, while a short personal note (or preferably, a verse) can be better than an actual pat on the back. People treasure personal praise in any form.

Stopping by my corporate office one day, I heard a conversation which revealed that one of our dedicated CPAs had stayed at her desk all night the night before to attend to some urgent payroll needs, accomplishing much and saving the day. I picked up a fat rose, and left it on her desk with:

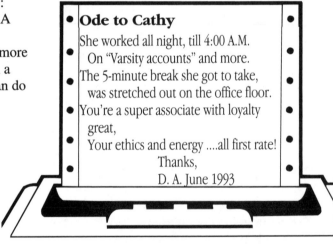

Ode to Cathy
She worked all night, till 4:00 A.M.
  On "Varsity accounts" and more.
The 5-minute break she got to take,
  was stretched out on the office floor.
You're a super associate with loyalty great,
  Your ethics and energy ....all first rate!
      Thanks,
      D. A. June 1993

I noticed that for months it was pinned in a prominent spot on her desk. A plain thank-you would have been tossed.

Most of my writing is done on the road, by hand on notebook paper or late in the evening in my home office typewriter, when I'm tired. So many of my drafts need imagination and a fair amount of perspiration to "clean them up." Not long ago I finally got around to thanking the person who does most of this, my operations manager, Tobi Haynes.

A Timely Tribute to My Translator

Now it isn't lack of editing, or loss of the specifics
nor lack of brilliance, in Aslett's hieroglyphics.

He thinks so fast that often neither keys nor pen can etch it
and adding or omitting a word or two, means she must work to
* catch it.*

Why tis just a little thing to spell "decide" <u>sekipL</u>
No reason at all for Tobi to wrinkle her brow: "Oh, hell..."

She puzzles over a sentence, every page or two
'cause I call everyone "Ol Horselips," she has to guess just who.

She needs some patience with "etc." and the way I spell ("ezbra")
* breeze*
and she never understands how much I love my parentheses (((()))!

Occasionally at 80 WPM my fingers lose the home keys—
she thinks I'm writing Russian, I hear her praying "Please..."

Why by now she ought to understand that <u>dsai</u> is always "said,"
<u>boother</u> is "both", and <u>drethe</u> is actually ... "dead."

The nerve that woman has, her approach is rather rough
yesterday she embarrassed me cause I couldn't translate my own
* stuff.*

But when the job is finished, oh how it pleases me
that woman's secret is, she does it by telepathy!
*   —DA July 97*

Whenever you can, put those well-deserved recognitions in poetry!

Poetry for AWARD-GIVING

Poetry can fit anywhere, and one good place is in award ceremonies. I've seen hundreds of awards given, for everything from government workers excelling to college presidents retiring, from bowling team and shooting team champions being singled out to Little League volunteers being recognized for length of service. There are usually the same old things written on those gold or silver trophies or mounted on those wood placques (name, date, company or division and title of award, period). Nothing creative here—this is just standard "shopsmith" recognition.

A thoughtfully constructed verse or rhyme, serious or humorous, can do the job a lot better—make the awardee feel special and everyone else realize and remember what the award was actually for.

Award poetry should be carefully prepared ahead. You don't want a poem that will distract from or dampen the award itself, serious or humorous. The award is the subject—don't get off the subject and steal the focus from the awardee at their big moment.

LOVE POEMS

There are basically only two "big ones" in life, by way of purposes or accomplishments. One is TO LOVE the other is TO BE LOVED. If you don't give and get your share of both of these, it seems to me that the rest of life is just a waste of white shirts and shower water.

No argument, the best poems around are those that capture and express pure love, for someone or something, a country or a cause. One of the great messages of the freedom of the soul was written by Richard Lovelace, a cavalier during the English Civil War. He was imprisoned and wrote to whom he loved. Look at the power in this last stanza.

Althea from Prison

Stone walls do not a prison make,
Nor iron bars a cage;
Minds innocent and quiet take
That for an hermitage;
If I have freedom in my love
And in my soul am free,
Angels alone, that soar above,
Enjoy such liberty.

In college, in my personal reading, and in the early days when my mother read great poems to me, I've read or heard most of the masters' best poems on "love"— Shakespeare, the cavalier poets, The Brownings, Lord Byron, Christina Rosetti, Edna St. Vincent Millay, and dozens of others. True, they had their touch. But today, fifty years further down the long road of life, I must admit I've seen equal if

not better from people like you, who did their own "outline of love" in verse.

There are so many of us and so much writing around now, that the chances of getting into the literature book alongside Longfellow and the rest are slim, but **getting alongside of them isn't our goal**. What we want to do is get in touch with ourselves and those we care about with our own expressions of love and feeling. Your own writing does in all logic and reality have more effect on life today, especially your own, than any collection of the masters.

When I went to find a sample of a love poem, I found that I've written numerous humorous poems of our family life, about shared experiences from cooking and kids, house to farmyard, but only a few feeling verses. This one, jotted in some moments of great appreciation for my wife, I did find tucked away.

The One Somewhere

Though my vacant praise might seem
 forever,
Weary I of you, dear, never,
While certain alterations of you I might
 frame
My reason to love you stays the same.
While schedule hours strip mind from feet
only with you I rest, and am complete.
Answering to others, you think me en-
 twined?
With them a little, with you it's a bind.
All my wisdom of life's sense of worth
Finds you second to no one I know on
 earth.

And one of my more recent little ditties (to come full circle to another "fourth grade valentine verse"):

Valentine Candy

The motel was dark as I lumbered in, again
away from home.
I threw my bags on the chair and sprawled
out on the foam.
Alone and lonesome again in that business
travel race.
Preparing to teach at yet another school as I
unpacked the ol' suitcase.
Nestled under a pair of socks I found a
package of candy hearts,
Niftily smuggled there by Barbs to remind
me, we weren't apart.
Although not fond of sweets the fact they
were lying there,
Gave me the most prestige in Texas, that
the wife I have does care.

Here is another example of a "verse
right from the heart," from another average
person just like you and me—a love poem
to inspire us to take the time to write our
own.

BIRTHDAY VERSES

Did you ever stop to think that out of
all the holidays and "celebration" days in
the year, there are only a couple of really
personal ones. And of those, birthdays are
unquestionably #1. What could acknowledge this yearly milestone better than a
sincere, personal letter, note, or—you
guessed it—a little verse. You can keep it
light and short, if you like, but avoid the
temptation of:

Gee, today you're looking nifty
Too bad you're old, fat, and fifty!

—being cruel instead of funny. Of course
just about any truly personal message beats

The Gift Inside

When the postman brings a package
Addressed direct to me,
With some unfathomed gift inside
Prepared so thoughtfully.

Is the ardor of the moment less
Because the box is worn?
Dog-eared and scuffed from its
   journey long,
And maybe a little torn?

No, I care not a whit for the outer
   wrap,
That corrugated cardboard skin.
I can hardly wait to get it off,
And see what lies within.

Behold our packages now, my dear,
These shells that hold us in.

I see some lumps and bulges where
Before was only thin.

The hair once dark is flecked with gray
and I need a longer belt.
Lines crease our faces like a map,
From the joy and pain we've felt.

So do I love you less, my sweet,
My gift from God above?
Is it just the shape of the outer shell
The determines my depth of love?

Nay...when our bodies become brand new,
Returning to God above,
The you inside will be the same.
The one I've come to love.
                              —Mark Browning.

92

an overpriced store-bought birthday card with someone else's verse on it.

When a colleague of mine expressed his awe of reaching fifty and asked me for "some wisdom for the fifties," I jotted this down and sent it. He loved it!

Some Half-Century Sense

Aging up to now, well really was it so?
But it's here at last for you, the sneaky Big Five-O.

You winked at 30, and 40 rationalized.
But when 50 arrives, you'd better wake up and rise.

Time runs out on dreams and plans and on our future wishin'
Man, this is serious stuff, there's got to be a mission.

So remember:
1. Two thirds of your life has already been spent on empty financial cravings
It's time at last to try, plain old common **savings**.

2. You've worked long enough for "gain," it's stupid to hustle wealth.
At 50 the only thing that really counts is superb **lasting health.**

3. For 49 years it was fine and social to just be "one of the guys"
Now you want to pursue and anchor those irreplaceable **family ties**.

4. As for all that stuff you kept to "sort" or possibly even wear
A wiser lifestyle now says **dump the majority of what's there.**

5. And for those hard-line positions you took and couldn't budge,
This is a good time to **lose all or any grudge**.

6. You've known there is a God, but still you don't know him.
It's **now or never** or the outlook's plenty grim.

7. And yes this is the final season of your lustrous **career**
If you still want to do it, do it now, for tomorrow may disappear.

8. Don't forget **your parents**, twenty years advanced on you,
Their golden years are your last vital ones too.

Mid-life is not a time to wait, to while, to sit.
But to repent, renew, redo, and now **get on with it!**

—DA December 7, 1995

SOME AREAS TO BE CAREFUL WITH

It's a free country, you have the right to write about whatever you want, but there are some areas that bear caution. We never want to hurt or offend anyone with a too clever or too invasive verse. Whenever we pick up a pen, even our best rhymes may be judged awkward or corny by others. That's OK, they're entitled to their opinion. But when our words are directed at someone in a sensitive situation, their intent or taste could be judged worse than corny. There are a few areas, for instance, where it may be hard to come up with something appropriate: one is weddings and the other anniversaries.

For your **own** wedding or anniversary, I believe anything goes, mushy or meek, sedate or racy (as long as it's well suited to the partner you're addressing it to). But when it comes to a wedding or anniversary verse for others, I'd be careful. We can take liberties within our own relationships, but the relationships of others are totally private. Any efforts to define or comment on them may well be judged intrusive. If you come up with a verse that hits the mark gracefully when it comes to the loves of others, let me know, I'd like to include it when I revise this volume.

AVOID THE LEWD AND CRUDE

There have undoubtedly been some great off-color and obscene poems written. We've all seen some on the walls of restrooms that were pretty clever, we have to admit, even though we may be put off by their crudeness. Once in a while, even the noblest of us will find a mood when something lewd or crude just works, a cussword that was custom made for some slot of rhyme and need for impact, an off-color or "bathroom" allusion that is just too witty to pass up. It's almost impossible to resist using...but **rarely are you wise to use it.**

Don't! You'll regret it no matter how clever or ingenious the result. What is written stands for the ages, records clearly and exactly just what you said. Poetry once written can be copied and distributed by anyone and there it is with your name right on it. You may think it would be fun to shock those stuffy folks out there. Forget it! Not much is shocking anymore, especially in the "gross" department, and when you come to your senses you won't be pleased to be identified with something like this.

If you say the same thing, people forget, don't pay too much attention, or think you made a slip of the tongue because you were under the influence or angry. So they are pretty forgiving and forgetting. But when something like this is written, especially in verse where it is so easy to remember and repeat... you're dead on the page. Obscenity or other touchy or very personal subjects are **never** really in good taste in poetry... you can be stimulating, seductive, and powerful without being base.

APOLOGIZING in Verse

The more sincere and graceful we can make an apology, the better, and poetry is perfect for the purpose. (A poem can also tenderize the crow we may need to eat, and help us "stand tall while we crawl.")

You forget or break a date, for instance, and know the other party is pretty upset about it. I wouldn't suggest a litany of explanations or excuses necessarily—it may be better to compose a something that defuses, eases, or lightens the situation. A verse attached to a little gift offering might work even better:

Can you believe? I missed our date.
I'm sorry for this glitch in fate!
I know you fretted as you sat,
and I feel like a skulking rat.
But rest assured I will amend,
and future contact will attend.
If you will, my dearest Mandy,
Accept, enjoy this box of candy.

94

It might come out corny, but the fact that you took the time to compose it will carry a mighty message. An apology for something less than tragic or earthshaking can tolerate a little corniness.

Even the briefest effort of this sort can work wonders. I brought a perfect pineapple back from Hawaii once and cut it up and set it on the art layout table for my operations manager, Tobi, who was at the time taking four calls and handling a couple of clients. It sat there quite a while and another friend came in so I offered it to him, believing Tobi had never noticed it or didn't want it. When she finally did come licking her chops for the finest of the island… a bare plate. Needless to say, I got many reminders the rest of the day. Then fortunately, another pineapple I'd brought appeared in another vehicle from home and so I cut it up nicely and left it beside her computer with a note, not a plain old note but a thirty-second verse:

> May this little plate stimulate your
>   gorgeous little liver,
> I know it's late, but worth the wait, from
>   your Pineapple Indian giver.
> —DA

She kept the poem taped to her computer for months after the pineapple was long gone. If I'd tried for a long complicated verse, the pineapple would have been rancid by the time I was done, or another friend might have appeared and I'd end up giving her dessert away again!

Poetry to LIGHTEN AN UNPLEASANTRY

Is there anything that can make a trip to the dentist fun? Sure! Do some verse on

it. I grew up with the usual understanding that dentists got their training and degree from KGB torture camps. When I was a freshman in high school, this poem popped up, author unknown. It is the description of the dentist in most people's minds. It's amazing how this simple verse captures the whole picture!

Excruciating

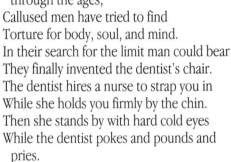

If you search
  through history's
  pages
You will find how
  through the ages,
Callused men have tried to find
Torture for body, soul, and mind.
In their search for the limit man could bear
They finally invented the dentist's chair.
The dentist hires a nurse to strap you in
While she holds you firmly by the chin.
Then she stands by with hard cold eyes
While the dentist pokes and pounds and
  pries.
The only time she really beams,
Is when he stuffs in cotton to still your
  screams.
When at last the tenderest spot he finds
He pokes and punches, hacks and grinds.
Till if you want to live, you start to doubt.
Then he gives you a shot so you can't black
  out.
He knows the quickest and easiest ways
To make you sick for days and days.
The torture's hell, but the worst durn sin,
You pay for the chair, fore they let you get
  in.

Having dodged the dentist for years, I was well into adulthood when a cookie in my shirt pocket picked up a crumb of concrete and cracked a tooth. I asked around and everyone agreed—the dentist I wanted was Dr. Max Johnson. He was the best and not expensive for the result he gave.

After checking over my teeth, he took me into a little room and explained the importance of the mouth and of keeping it well and practicing some preventive maintenance. It was the best and most influential two hours I'd ever spent, even counting my two full previous years in college. I learned that the health of the mouth was connected with the health of the body in general, and I began to floss and cut down on sugar. My life changed—the once-a-year flu and strep I always counted on and other related downs have for the last thirty years been eliminated from my life. Dentists are among our best friends!

Then I was guided in to a lovely brown-eyed hygienist named Kay Beach, who ran me through a five-visit course in enlightened tooth care. I was so impressed I versed it, a summary of the six visits. I'll give you a verse out of each.

First visit: "Mr. Aslett, do you brush the
  teeth that God has given you?"
I could not lie to a big brown eye, so I said,
  "Well yes, every week or two."

Second visit: "Here you missed, there you
  missed, "Where" was professionally said.
There wasn't a tooth completely cleaned,
  my ego was totally dead.

Third visit: "Not bad at all, but do you want
  to keep these four teeth in back?
Yipes, in the light they were far from white,
  how did I miss them in my brush attack?

Fourth visit: For this visit, I was psyched. I
  brushed my teeth to death,
I brushed my tongue and every crown,

subduing all dog breath.

Fifth visit: My mouth marathon this time
  she lauded, and did it with a smile.
I finished first, she assured me, I'd beat the
  four-molar mile.

Now I didn't get my diploma, not a trophy
  for the class.
Cause I haven't yet been to visit six. But I
  know I'll pass!
I know another thing, too, beside my teeth
  are saved.
I'll get another toothbrush, for being so well
  behaved.

Everyone in that office has treated me like family since, so a thank-you or acknowledgment in verse, perfect or not, passes!

I'm a firm believer that poetry can lighten and brighten even the worst of situations. For example, have you ever stripped the built-up wax off a floor? It's a gutty job and always takes longer than you think, and the fumes and slipperiness are twice as bad as you are ever prepared for. Many years ago now my professional cleaning crew and I were given an old, old, floor to strip in the Rock Springs, Wyoming, telephone company building. We were working upstairs in the traffic department, where all the operators were that gave out information and numbers. They had to stay at their posts (headsets) while we took a quarter inch of old wax off the floor. It was tougher on them than us. After we finished the job, my partner Arlo bought some flowers and I wrote a poem and got an employee to sketch up a card with it and we gave to the operators with the flowers. It only took minutes to do and it blew the ladies away.

To The Rocksprings Traffic Gals

※ These flowers are for...

Dorothy, whose radiance and glow, within the traffic door,
        inspired us to produce the gloss shine on the floor!!
        And the 3 women who got glued to the locker room floor
        and hung from fixtures for safety from the wax mop's soar!
        And that sweet little redhead who worked all through the
        night
manning her station in spite of the plight...
while handling 9 customers, not once did they suffer
as she dispatched her calls perched atop of our buffer!

And let's not forget Numa, she drew us each shift,
& 16 grubby janitors is certainly no gift!

And specially the women who   really had to "go"
but they waited for the restroom   as we cleaned it high
                             & low.

In fact... to all the ladies, who as the calls came in,
were cheery, polite, & helped our work
over and over again.

We realize your terror as
the dirt was swept away
... and we sure want to thank you;
YOU REALLY MADE OUR DAY!!!

Thank you!
The Varsity Crew

They all made copies and hung it up at home. We were delighted and the word (a good word) got back to our telephone company boss… Poetry blesses our lives in many ways.

Expediency is the key here. Don't wait too long to acknowledge the situation you want to lighten. Waiting always lets memory dull and prejudice take a firm hold. A quick verse will get you much more mileage than a delayed masterpiece.

Make the Point in POETRY Instead

Poetry forces you to sift things and boil them down, be precise, cut the excess.

Thus a few verses can often cover what would otherwise take pages and pages.

When I do TV appearances and media tours for my books on clutter, for example, people are always interested in how we Americans compare with other countries when it comes to how much "stuff" we have kicking around. I was going to write a section on this to include in my next book on dejunking, and then I decided that doing it in rhyme would take half the time and space. Though not a masterpiece, the following does make the comparison better than several pages of dull paragraphs (I thought so anyway).

UN Clutter

The question was, "Do they have
as much, as we in the USA?"
Piles of junk, and clutter too—all
that stuff that's in our way.
All I can tell, as I travel, well, only here do
we have the room.
In Japan, each house has maybe one fan,
and only a single broom.

In our dwellings here, we have room to
spare, maybe even a second place.
While living quarters, south of our borders,
may be smaller than our closet space.
Here in the States, we collect plates, and
even display them (it's kind of rude).
In Russia they compete just for something
to eat, the focus is all on the food.

While we rent storage for broken lamps and
cushionless couches
In the Himalayan hills, they find thrills, in
what can be carried in small back pouches.
We have so much, we can hardly touch,
without some navigational planning.
Longer and better do the Polynesians live,
with time to enjoy sun tanning.

So we live clutter heaped, with extra
everything, and all kinds of fine enamel,
While Arabs move about, and well make
out, with nothing but a tent and camel.
And in China and Korea, where they make
junk, that is sold for plenty yen,
Why glory be, they are clutter free, because we
buy it all from them.

Why did we get all this, too much! Were we
just putting on the Ritz?
I've heard it said, 'twas descended and bred, It
came directly from the "Brits."
That's not quite fair because "over there"
some piles may be higher and quainter
But they've been collecting for centuries
longer and the call of the mall is fainter.

We came to acquiring late, but applied
ourselves so enthusiastically
The only question seems to be "who has more
than me?"
The land of the free soon meant the land of
MORE
We became a world leader in clutter, too—the
proof is just inside our door.

Writing About Everyday Subjects

You can have a lot of fun with verse, writing about the most common, ordinary subjects.

Let's take one of the most "everyday" subjects of all, food. I was surprised at the amount of poetry on this subject I had in the old file. Eating is not a big thing with me. I can miss two or three meals in a row without remembering. Yet I'm very aware of how much time and money most people spend on food, and how often food is focused on before other, far more important things. My food poems are often negative, but yours could be enthusiastic celebrations of fresh-picked sweet corn or ice cream sundaes.

Here are just a few samples of the possibilities of food poems, mean to inspire you to express yourself after the next trip to a restaurant, grocery store, or the refrigerator!

How many other odes to hot dogs do you think there are around?

Likewise, since I raised pigs professionally for years, I thought I had the right to comment on one of their products.

Bacon

It robbed a pig of sacred life
Was soaked and cured prior to the knife
then a hot grease bath, while paper thin,
Gasp, I'll never eat dead pig again.
—DA 1980

I hold a more respectful view of another cholesterol maker and one day preparing to eat a packed lunch, I was impelled to write about a couple of boiled eggs. Maybe I was just desperate for a verse subject, but look how differently and creatively you can present an egg.

The Airport Hot Dog

A "vow" you'll never do it again
we've made plenty of these for sure.
Not to say, eat, or do something stupid
or other wise impure.

I promised myself that never again,
no matter how desperate I might be
would I lower myself to the pantry shelf
of an airport eatery.

It was 7 years since that last hot dog,
a meal that shortened breath.
But amazing how time and hunger heals
the fear of digestive death.

But two meals I'd missed, and the outlook bad
for food along the way.

Tis said every man does have his price,
And this was a hungry day.

I shouldn't have stopped at that grill
of dogs rolling in shiny grease,
or noticed others eating them
none of whom looked deceased.

So I ordered up to try again,
a road I'd gulped before.
One more chance, with a nervous glance,
I wolfed down that tube of gore.

Now here I sit, on the verge of tears
my system out on strike,
Wondering if in five more years
I'll repeat this Maalox plight.
—DA November 1990

Boiled Eggs in My Lunch

There they laid, peekin' out between a tuna and a jam,
Two Leghorn's labors, and in eight minutes they were damned.

The challenge of preparation, before they nourish me,
Is to find that last part of shell I didn't see.

The fatal decision then I make—which end of it to bite,
The off center yolk mocks me now, threatening tasteless plight.

For who likes all yolk? I don't, nor all white as a matter of fact,
So from the side I draft a plan and steer my snack attack.

Soon egg one is gone and enjoyed without its cover,
The second I just eat, as do most egg lovers.
—DA 1972

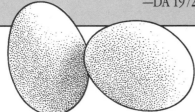

Before you "chicken" out on reading more, try something as plain as mush.

Oatmeal Inflation

About the recent price raise
I've maintained a polite hush
But now, I'm not too happy
About the change in breakfast mush.
For the last week while in the restaurant
When I ordered up oatmeal
The dish brought up to my table
Was a $3 deal.
Ten bites it took to consume it
That figures 30 cents a munch
And hardly a stable nutrient
To last me until lunch.
And remembered I, the good ol' days
When the price was less unnerving
And cereal piping hot was sold
For less than five cents a serving.

This last "food poem" was on a subject others have commented on and after I did this it was copied and passed to quite a few congregations!

Cheerios (Heavenly Donuts) in Church

To keep the darlings
  hushed at church
Parents for ages made a
  search.

And finally discovered the neatest material
Boxed and sold as breakfast cereal.

A handful of Cheerios sure beats a stare
To cut off sniffs and howls during prayer.

While parents provide that round little snack
The spoiled little feasters rattle the sack.

The other kids who just have a hymn book
Drool on the bench from the smell and a
  look.

The trouble I see from this worshipful treat,
Is that half of it ends up under the seat.

It's tracked on the rug and out the front door,
And have you ever cleaned these sticky "o's"
  off the floor?

Those church-lunching parents are much out
  of line
For no scripture commands or permits such
  crime.

In heaven, may these offenders rise on their
  toes
And live in a kingdom of wet Cheerios.
—DA 1980

You could hardly find a more mundane, "everyday" subject than what this next poem focuses on—that grimy crack in the kitchen between counter and stove.

> The gentleman who designed my previous
> kitchen is unknown to me and nameless
> Which does not mean I hold him blameless.
> For he decreed that there should be a gap
> just one inch wide
> Between the stove and the bench it stood
> beside.
> The gruesome things that can drip, drop,
> dribble, and drain down such a region
> Are legion.
> Who knows what horrid creatures wallow
> In this dank disgusting hollow?
> If there is justice at all in the Afterlife
> This guy has sure earned lots of strife.
> Such as row upon row of tiny abysses
> Between the benches and the cooking
> dishes.
> Which he's forced to scrub with a tiny brush
> While his probing fingers twist and crush
> In ungettable nooks and crannies
> In which the bacon fat can fall
> And little beasties creep and crawl.
> —Roslyn Taylor

Clothes Poems

Let's take something more personal now, our clothes, wearing apparel. Some of our clothes become quite dear to us, if we were to be honest about it. They make us look good, keep us warm or cool, and we were wearing them when we got promoted or won the heart or the Cadillac. The best of them deserve more than to hang around and be turned into rags someday. We've all had a dress, a coat, a hat, or something that was dear to us. I had a suit that was iron loomed, perfectly fitting, and forgiving to a fault. I loved it, but after twelve years of constant wear it was unquestionably a "senior suit." So I wrote:

The Faithful Suit

> You bought it, luckily, and
> paid a lot.
> It grew on you to the best
> you've got.
> It did its thing for years,
> was great,
> Now it's old and out of
> date.
>
> But it won't die and wear won't show,
> And it's adapted, that you know.
> Another suit you need to get
> Won't this garb ever quit?
>
> Well, one more time before it's tossed.
> You wear it again, a promise lost.
> It still looks good, there are no sags,
> What decent dude would make it rags?
>
> Okay, one more cleaning and toot-a-loo,
> But back it comes, good as new.
> Though I can afford to robe a king,
> I guess I'll just keep this slick old thing.
> —DA April 1996

Sometimes you just plain need a poem to start or end something—entering or exiting from it without expressing your feelings in some way seems hard to do. This can even be true of the most mundane things.

I've always been a work boot, not a loafer man, for example—fancy or exotic shoes just aren't my thing. But now that I spend a good part of the year in Hawaii, where everyone takes off their shoes at the door and there is a lot of nice sand to soothe the toes, I finally succumbed to a pair of sandals. First I tried the thong between the toes type (which was surely invented by a third world torture commit-tee). I finally settled on the simple strapped slip-on, but even those had their problems. For six years I suffered with them, limping around trying to look relaxed. One day after two falls, a stubbed toe, and a puddle encounter—that was enough! It was time to give up and re-shoe. I'd failed to master those stupid soles, so I had to verse it to get revenge. I tacked one of the sandals onto a tree for a month with this eulogy:

Sandal Scandal

I gave you a chance, you rubber buggers,
Never again will you be one of
    my foot huggers.

No speed of change can justify
The agony you've caused this traveling guy.

I've cramped my toes for a tighter grip
To avoid losing you on a walking trip.

With no protection, I've stubbed my toes
And collected pieces of all that grows.

That open top just welcomes soot
And who really wants to view a bony foot?

I'm sick of your drag and noisy flaps,
The scraping shuffle from those plastic
    straps.

Today is the end, I'm through keeping tabs
On you miserable, cheap, slippery slabs!

I feel no remorse tossing these losers,
Tis not my style these Jerusalem cruisers.

—DA Hawaii 1996

Poetry as WEAPON OR COMEBACK

I'm not suggesting that the best use of poetry is as a weapon, but it can and does work. How often we can make little swipes with it that really fit the occasion. I remem-ber our coach in college once giving us the big pep talk of the season on the value of training and conditioning. He ended his great address with the old familiar: "Re-member, early to bed and early to rise, makes a man healthy, wealthy, and wise." One of the more creative jocks in the back of the locker room piped up, "Yeah, but remember coach, early to bed and early to rise and your girl goes out with other guys."

That brought a roar of laughter from even the coach and it became kind of a corollary in the training rules. If your girl was going out with or left you for someone else, then you must be keeping the rules!

I remember my mother saying to my little brother in the same health lecture mode:

"Remember, Larry, an apple a day keeps the doctor away."

His third-grade reply was, "and I bet too much cake, keeps the doctor awake!"

Well said, as can only be done by poetry and rhyme!

Lots of verse makers have found that war making can be done better with a poem than a confrontation. We can com-plain, bitch, and moan over an injustice and it often goes unheard—it's ignored or surely not long remembered. But a poem, verse, or lyric will get a much better lick in. A sarcastic poem beats a raised fist any day.

My wife and I have never struck each other in forty years of marriage. In fact we don't even fight and argue. In our next forty years together, we might resort to a good old wrestling match someday. But right now, we both have more class than that. When disagreements or irritations temporarily overshadow tranquillity and compatibility, I retreat to a corner and write a sarcastic poem. She retreats to the laundry room and seizes my clean undergarments and goes out in the field and drags them through the weeds and burrs. The following day, I begin itching and ouching as the stickers make their presence known. Then I am reminded or become aware that I said or did something wrong. Retaliating by poem, I feel, has more dignity than "sticker dragging underwear." The pen is mightier than the barb any day.

In my file of little whippers from "the thistle wars," I found one I'd written called, "It Really Frosted Me." The day it was written, we'd just finished building our new ranch house and had a master cabinet-maker build some beautiful birch cabinets in the kitchen. They were magnificent, but the space left for the refrigerator was a bit tight—only 39 3/4 inches wide. Shopping for the new fridge, Barbara called me at my office. She'd found this really nice family fridge which was 40 inches wide. "It won't fit, Dear, buy a smaller one—those cabinets are like concrete." "But it's on sale." "Buy a smaller one, Dear." Well you know women's logic when it comes to practicalities like building structure, they are idealists, especially when something is on sale. She bought it, and fitting a 40-inch appliance into an unyielding 39 3/4 inches was an effort even then truly worthy of a poem. May I excerpt a few lines?

One side of the cabinet was a foot of birch,
The other was stone, firm as a century-old church.
"If it doesn't fit," says one (ignoring the measure rule),
"We can sand 1/4 inch off the stone by the kitchen stool."
"Perhaps a miracle," said the other, "and it will slide right in.
And that 1/4 inch will disappear right off the casing then.
And maybe we can beat on it and squeeze that steel fridge a bit
Or scrape off a .013 millimeter of paint and make it easily fit.
Maybe we can lard it up with Crisco or some butter,
And fool the quarter inch, twill slide in without a shudder."
—DA 1965

She didn't give up, however, and somehow—by bowing the wall, sanding, and praying, that massive refrigerator was hammered and lodged in there, and there it stayed for the next thirty years. Don't ask me where the 1/4 inch went, either, all I know is that a woman pulled it off again.

Let's look at a few examples now from the business world.

A great treat in life (often a treatment!) is working with a professional editor, especially in your infancy of writing. If you had or have any self-confidence, self-esteem, or love for the words you wrote, you better loosen up because you literally end up on a chopping block. It's hard to take because even when the work seems perfect and all your friends and relatives are raving about it, the manuscript can come back beaten to a pulp. Following one unmerciful attack on my best work, I did the only retaliation move I could muster, a verse rebuttal. I wrote as if the manuscript was a human.

They'll delete you,
  red mark you
    With faces like tombs,
    Then attach twenty flags to
      the sides
    When they run out of
      criticism room.
    Poor thing, you can't breathe
      now
    The structure is so tight,
    You have no character
      because
    Every word is spelled just
      right.
                —DA 1982

Moving to the realm of personal appearances and publicity, I sent this poem to one of my Home Show sponsors with a request for a quieter place to perform. (It did the trick, too!)

I worked for a famous tennis pro once who always came out on top in every deal, he found a way to work everything to his advantage. I found no way to express my frustration except verse, so I wrote him a two-page epistle making a rhyme of every time he'd gouged me. Here are a few stanzas from it:

Now when Wilkins offers to make a deal
  that will really make you great
Translated, he wants your help, which
  you're expected to donate.

His best friends are like chessmen when-
  ever a project's on
He moves Simon against Harry, then
  Clayton against Don.

When he offers you a drink and you think
  you've got it made,
All you get is a paper cup, filled with Gator
  Aid.

He'll invite you to supper and ask "What do
  you like?"
You'll slave free for hours, and then to his
  house hike.

A Home Show Slant (after surviving over 500 home show performances)

You put me next to grinding wheel rims,
two home theaters, and a kiddie play gym.
Twenty head microphones and whirling
  mixers,
Vacuums roaring and the rattling of fixtures.
Barking of dogs, hot tubs a-flushing,
Riveting frogs and garden walls gushing.
Vegetable chopping, noisy cement floors
Motors, sanders, and banging back doors.
Food service ice and Indian urns
and a singing model of old Fred Burns.
Roasters, stereos, and thirty TVs,
competing in volume with piano keys.
Right under air handlers with twenty-foot
  fans
Next to the dumpster and all the garbage
  cans.
My audience straining to hear a voice sound
when right next to a merry-go-round.
I love performing and I also love you
But I cannot survive in such a zoo!
                —DA end of the season, 1997.

There is a note saying, "Help yourself to the
delicious steak."
But all I find is the clean saucer, from which
Ol' Spike just ate.

I paint his shop and clean his rug and all
that he can choose
to honor me with is a tournament prize,
one of his old used tennis shoes.

The thing I can't believe, that puts me in
high gear
Is that racket wizard gets me every single
year.
—DA 1969

For the head man at a telephone
company in a midwestern area, my cleaning company contracted to put in the
landscaping and the sprinkler system, on a
tight, tight budget. He only had so much
money, but wanted ever more done for it.
We always try to accommodate our customers, so he gradually talked us into more
and more work for less and less pay. The
bottom line of the job was well expressed
in the last line of a poem I wrote and sent
him with the bill.

Neal rubbed his hands, the contractor
crippled home,
Would their stocks drop to the bottom?
This we won't know till statement day,
But we know Neal really "got em."

His home high school team was the
Delta Rabbits, and in a later stanza I was
able to use the rabbits to great advantage to
help describe his efforts to get four times
the work done for the same money.

Another case where I got a serious
message across by poking fun. You can do
that with a poem. A few months later
another job came up (a good, high-profit
one) and he called and gave it to us with a
chuckle.

One can chop and cut pretty deep with
the old rhyme ax. Avoid mean verse, if you
can manage to resist it. Read something ten
times and sit on it a week before issuing it
forth to the world. Most verse done when
you are riled is not that good, and it can
take forever to live down something really
nasty.

If you plan to use a poem to stick a
knife into someone, try to do it subtlely so
the recipient doesn't feel anything till later.
Keep out the fighting words like "better,"
"never," "must," "always," "mine," "or
else," and "should," Don't threaten, just
thread your poem with some suggestions
and let them make their own interpretation:

One can be a horse's butt, aggravating and
heady,
One can be a thief or sloth, for work never
be ready.
One can be a radical, emotionally unsteady,
But none of these can match the sin, of
simply being petty.
—DA May 97

Using Poetry to
ADVANCE A CAUSE

Much, MUCH poetry (probably almost
as much as is sentimental and love motivated) is done for a cause, a purpose, some
issue of right or freedom, in short something serious.

Poems can be a polite way to "preach."
Say you have a cause or a cure. Few listen
because you have to march, shout, and
whine for justice along with all those

hundreds and thousands of other reformers out there. Long, complaining, threatening, alarmist treatises are seldom published, and seldom read, even when they are. Poetry can present a hard message in a softer way. If you take those crowded pages of fine print and put the message in poetry instead, I bet twice as many would read it, and five times as many would remember it, and even mention it to friends.

For example, the city or county is widening a road and is about to cut down a dozen beautiful eighty-year old trees. Many are displeased and they sign petitions, write full-column letters to the editor about it, etc. Far better instead to find one of you who can reduce the argument to rhyme:

Do we want to see those bulldozers chug
Through lover's lane where we kissed and hugged?
Replacing foliage with an asphalt siege.
Removing spirit and some heritage.
Surely we can go around
and not disturb that sacred ground.
Lose all that beauty and cooling shade
Along with those oaken sentinels staid.
Let's think again before we see
Those beautiful trees turned to debris.

Or consider the following couplet, a far more piercing commentary than could be achieved in pages of prose complaining about the excesses of "the space race."

While in the race to save our face
Why don't we conquer inner space?

Try a poem for your next mission, instead of an assembly!

Poetry in POLITICS

Here is an area where no one can deny the influence of verse—the effect, good or bad, that a few little rhyming words can have on politics, war, or peace. Politicians have long won or lost, been made or undone by clever slogans. Someone comes up with a catchy phrase or rhyme with their politician's message and—bingo—every kid in town is singing or saying it and adult whistling it. "I like Ike" was a three-word rhyme that worked. While I was in college one of our local Pocatello politicians came up with, "Go all the way with Vernon K," and by the time we citizens had heard it several times, many of us forgot who else was even in the race.

We all remember the history book rhyme "Tippicanoe and Tyler, too" that helped propel John Tyler to the presidency. The anti Vietnam war rhyme "LBJ, LBJ, How many kids have you killed today?" lent some real force to the anti-Vietnam War effort, and the rhyming nickname "Tricky Dick" had a part in the downfall of Richard Nixon.

During a book publishing tour, I was privileged to work a full day and evening with political satirist Mark Russell. Like fifty other high-profile political newscasters, talk show hosts and analysts, he has lots of political opinions for the public. But he delivers his not in headlines, in forum settings, or from a podium, but standing behind a red, white, and blue grand piano and putting all his barbs, summaries, and messages into sung poetry. His clever verses have audiences leaning in for the next line and laughing and clapping when it comes. A mighty effective way to stick the politicians and make sure his messages stick with listeners. Leave out the rhyme and verse and he'd be just one more dry political commentator.

Just for fun, the next time your political hero or heroine runs, pretend you are the "campaign manager" and do a verse for him or her or their message. I'll bet it'll be so good you'll mail it to them!

Putting Your PHILOSOPHY OF LIFE in Verse

Ever thought about putting your philosophy of life in a verse? Do it, try it. I've always told people my goal is to die with a shining shovel, but that doesn't explain it well to most. So when Barbara Walters pins me down with "what rules do you play by in life?", she is going to get my answer in verse:

A WATCHER I don't
   want to be
To USE what's there is
   dull to me,
Just a READER of
   another's page
Or being ENTERTAINED
   is an insult to my age.
Let me DO while others look
And WRITE, not use that HOW-TO BOOK,
No waiting for the End with Doubt
I WANT THE STAGE... till time runs out.
       —DA Honolulu 1981

Again, don't hesitate to put your feelings down on paper… your philosophies, code of ethics, and your direction in life. Few people ever write down their goals, but there is something about writing them out and re-reading them from time to time that helps keep us on course and on target.

Those who do spell out what they want from life seem better directed and more content—they know where they are going, so they enjoy the trip and are fully aware of when they get there. Even better than just jotting a few lines or lists of boundaries, wishes, wants, and promises to yourself and others, put it in a verse.

The following poem is one I wrote almost forty years ago now, but it's still one of my guidelines today. Don't we know ourselves better than anyone else?

A Code of Ethics of a Personal Nature

May nothing made of earth's mined core,
Escort my mind away from what it's for,
May my "job" never dominate the goal it
   seeks to achieve,
May compensation gained not cause my wit
   to leave.
May positions attained in time, not attain
   me,
May praise and help, help my soul better
   see.
May those I love take from me, until I feel
   the fast,
May I continue to gain wealth that this
   supply will last.
May my home show beauty in what it yields
   to all,
May the warmth therein be from the heart,
   not just the walls.
May the collections there be for use and not
   display,
May any child feel at ease among the best I
   do weigh.
Free may my apparel be of glamour's ghost,
May it practice thrift, so my rags won't have
   to boast.
May I always have the time to shun the
   chores, when life calls louder,
May my life book always show the balance—
   whether greed or heart is stouter.
       —DA 1963

OPINION Poems

Aren't they all?

It may not be an official classification, but there is definitely a species or group of lyrics called opinion poems. Sometimes these may not accomplish anything in the outside world in the end, but it still feels good to get the sentiments involved out of your system, onto a page or into a verse. It beats all to heck expressing them at some loud party or in a casual conversation. If poetry served no other purpose than to get frustrations off our chest, it would be valuable.

For example: We've all used those plastic earphones that provide the sound for movies on an airplane flight. My ears always ached and were warped for at least two hours after the movie, but I was still dumb enough to use them again and again. One time as the flight attendants came by before the movie offering them for the usual inflated price, I wrote instead of rented:

Airline Earphone

Beginning with a liability
Of roaring jets right next to me
Just five minutes off the ground
They sell that plastic tubing sound.
Designed to fit no human ear
Why do I engage that torture gear?
Grimacing in stethoscope poise,
I labor to transcribe that garbled noise.
Trying too often, on too many trips
I finally gave up, and now read lips!
                                    —DA November 1994

When I was finished, I relaxed and grinned.

Being a believer that silence is golden,

especially when doing mental work, another time I wrote:

While resting, thinking, without the crowd
I question the man whose nature is loud.
For how easily the tapping, clicking, chattering kind
Can disrupt the concert of the mind.
                                    —DA 1975

As "America's #1 Dejunker" and a professional cleaner whose company cleans about a hundred million square feet of office space every night, I get to see a lot of desks. Desks are always loaded with coffee cups, and more appear or are given to the owner each week. Following a TV segment I did in Wisconsin, I gave my opinion of the newsroom desk where I had to wait between takes.

The Mug

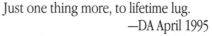

A ceramic cylinder fitting
    index finger
Designed and printed,
    remains to linger.
For charm or drink, they
    get our hug.
Just one thing more, to lifetime lug.
                                    —DA April 1995

And some spiritual opinion now. I was with a pious, righteous group of church people one day, all afternoon, who thought they had risen above plain old Christianity. I finally found them so intolerable I quoted to them the famous verse I read years ago and loved (author unknown), "Helping hands are holier than praying limbs."

They missed the point and so I did them a little opinion poem which they deserved. Here are a few stanzas from it:

108

Asleep at the Wheel

In search of lives that we may bless
How do we define "righteousness"?

So many won't miss an alm or prayer,
yet can leave their duty sitting there.

Give me a seasoned sinner any day
Over a sitting Saint amen-ing away.
—DA Baltimore, March 1991

We've all been through the "success training" syndrome, in which all kinds of "Go for the goal" people offer and teach rah-rah motivational seminars, at every convention, conference, and company meeting. Sitting through at least my twentieth of same with a room full of other sighers, hearing all that reused and worn-out stuff, I jotted down my stand.

Rah Rah Rot

Ah! more self-improvement seminars
On ways to heal all our scars.
A crowded room of girls and guys
Where we will be "quadrantized."
Learn to create charisma and remember
    names
communicate and play manner games.
Tips and traps and formulas,
"Containment" and commitment buzz.
Verbiage and drawings borrowed from
    each other
Seeing examples would be my druther.
—DA July 97

Building a home will expose you to enough bureaucracy (permits, county and city rules, and building codes) to last a lifetime, but then try developing some property. I had thirty acres on a cliff which I hadn't decided whether to make into five-acre estates or just plain old sagebrush

pasture (because we're in the country twenty miles out of town). I waded for weeks through all the "departments," but the Health department was the biggest hassle—the attitude, the service, etc. While my neighbor went in and threatened and screamed at them with a clenched fist and a hammer in the other hand, I choose a cutting verse to summarize the situation:

Specs for Health Department

To build some houses on a knoll,
    five acres per home allowed,
I couldn't proceed per the health
    code rules, until twenty-foot
    holes were plowed.
To guarantee the sewage flushed,
    that I wouldn't let a germ
    escape,
While a few feet of dirt and a
    regular tank would have kept
    things from smelling ape.
But a system capable of handling a
    New York hotel was specified
While 2000 cows without benefit
    of septic, crapped on the land on
    either side.

I still had to obey the rules, but at least now I felt better about it.

To provide a "living exhibit" for a best-selling book of mine on the subject, my wife and I are building a maintenance-free house up in the mountains of Kauai. There are some farms nearby, and one year a mysterious bull would come out at night and root around and poop all over and leave a trail of ruined trees and bushes on ours and other residential homesites. No one ever saw the bull, but many heard him bellowing and saw his calling card of destroyed landscape. The neighborhood was literally up in arms. No one managed to hunt him down, and when the police were called in, they couldn't apprehend what they couldn't find. I was away for a week in Canada, doing a home show and when I got a call from Hawaii, from my wife who was visiting there, I was in the mood for a romantic, loving conversation...

The hotel phone finally rang,
my heart began to race,
For only my loving wife has the
number of this place.
I snatched the phone breathing hard,
all prepared to snort,
It was her all right but what
I got was the daily
"bull" report.

After the call I hung up and instead of a letter wrote a little verse called, "No Bull," from which the lines above are an excerpt. My wife loved the poem and shared it with all the neighbors. Would an ordinary letter, no matter how well worded, have gotten shared with the neighbors?

The new electric insect control machine we added to our home in Hawaii one year did indeed cut down on the bugs. It was a pure positive until our favorite gecko ventured too close to it, an event too illuminating to pass up!

Free Lunch

You've all seen those zappers, made to kill
bugs—
All kinds of insects, mosquitoes, and flies.
Electronic bright, this shocking delight
You can hear and see with your eyes.

Dwelling nearby, with a glint in his eye
A gecko wise past his years,
Found if he stayed by the light where they
played
His meal always freely appeared.

Wow, this was a deal, a delivered meal!
He soon hung out on the unit
And nailed every moth, as it came forth,
Seemed nothing in the system could ruin it.

Yes, he had it made, there in the shade
But good lessons always come hard
In one of his scores, his tail twitched for
more
And landed under the guard.

The zapper lit up, but not with his sup
The gecko commenced being fried
So much for free lunch, it cost him a bunch
To the donor you'll always be tied!
—DA May 97

If you have a message, verse it. Strong opinion is fine in a poem, as long as it isn't preachy or judgmental (see page 110 on how to avoid "moralizing" in verse).

Using Poetry to CONQUER IRRITATIONS (or at least soothe them a little)

Some of us have pretty short fuses and raw nerves when we get tired or discouraged, and some of us are that way all the time. They call it high strung, hyper, or the like. It's often little things bother us, from people clipping fingernails in full view of everyone, to certain elevator music, or being paired with a horsebutt all day in a seminar, at work, or on the playing field. Things like this just plain get to you.

I've been accused of being a little less than tolerant of poor manners (just because I stop my lecture or speech when someone clicks a pen or rattles ice). I consider that the only thing to do, of course, even if others don't. Otherwise, my only salvation from irritations like this is to bristle inside and grab my pen and pad.

I travel to New York a lot and that is a real test of your immunity to bad manners. I've written an entire book, much of it in rhyme, just on manners, and the "Big Apple" is the perfect research place. I hit the back patters, belchers, borrowers, coin rattlers, car sitters, line crowders, ice eaters, and many more. Here's a little sampling:

The Cough

I can see a healthy cough,
And even a rousing sneeze
But spare me that constant barking and
  gasping
and sniffing on me please.
Coughing half in your hand,
and half on me
Surely "hacks" any dignity!

Pen Clickers

There I sat one afternoon in quiet meditation
Doing the office work I love with silent dedication.
When in a troop of associates seeking my wisdom filed
I bade them sit and fire away; my face it had a smile.

Before the first question was totally out, one of them began his pen to flick
His thumbs worked it wildly, that little ballpoint Bic.

Another began snapping his Schaefer on the other side of the room
I swear they were clicking a pen duet; those buggers were right in tune!

Then catching the spirit of the rhythm, a third one joined in
With a big Parker marker he added a bass, and jumped into the din.

A Speedwriter clasped in another's hand, added a tenor sound.
The last one there had no pen at all, so on his wristwatch he did pound.

There they were, all clacking away, like a chorus with clattery tools.
To this day they wonder why I kicked them out, those poor pen-clicking fools.

Ode to Seat Savers

In every auditorium, stadium, or assembly
  hall
Is the same bad-mannered enemy, brim-
  ming full of gall.

The self-appointed savior to those who
  can't tell time
Cheater of the honest, punctual folks,
  friends of yours and mine.

When he reaches any edifice, he races to
  the front
Claims seats with his coat and eight programs, for an opening stunt.

Then with his vacant kingdom plotted, he
  guards it from both ends
Reserving the seats, he claims, for some
  momentarily arriving friends.

Line after line of patrons spot the seats
  unoccupied.
And struggle gamely to collect their
  seeming seating prize.

Only to find that nervy squatter digging his
  fingernails in
Stretching over all nine seats he thinks
  belong to him.

The hall is now so packed, there is standing
  room only in the rear
Even to the crippled woman of ninety he
  says, "These seats are saved, my dear."

Finally, yes you guessed it, his friends show
  up at last
Just in time to interrupt the artist, and all
  the performing cast.

The seat saver jumps up and signals by
  waving his overcoat
And those latecomers climb to get their
  seats, like a band of mountain goats.

When those ill-mannered savers finally
  reach heaven's streets so nobly paved
I hope they hear St. Peter say, "I'm sorry,
  but those seats are saved."

You'll probably write most of your "irritant" poems for yourself. And it's worth it, folks—it sure beats punching a wall or yelling at the dog.

A Poet's Waterloo... MORALIZING

Well, I can see it,
why can't you
This world is rotten...
I think I'll sue!
  —1991

We all have a message, and not only for ourselves, our family and business, but the whole world. Admit it or not, most of us have some solutions for the woes of the world and everyone in it. Even those of you who don't say much, are right in there with those of us who often say too much. It is automatic and natural, the quest to get things off our chest, and it can slip into our verse in the blink of an eye.

It's fairly easy to moralize in conversation, much easier to moralize in essay writing, and not just super easy, but **a constant temptation** to moralize in verse. Once we get revved up into rhyme, we can really preach a rolling sermon to all those miserable souls out there who need reforming. Of course we all believe we are right—our course and direction, our choices and standards are the real and right ones, and anyone below or above our line is not quite with it and needs a little poem to point them in the right direction. Bill Brohaugh, a Writer's Digest editor, put it well in describing one of my own writings that had too much of a moral edge on it:

"You come across as saying 'Now that all of you people have screwed things up good, let me tell you how to fix it.' "

Any verse can stand a little "in the wicked world today" flavor, but too much is a turn-off. Moralizing is tabbed by most appreciators of poetry as the number one fault of we poets. We tend to use verse as a platform for lecturing about the "rights and wrongs" of life—as we see them. Sure we are entitled to opinion, and for that matter to our own set of ethics, but opinion turns into judgment so quick you won't believe it.

Often our very first "ode" in verse is inspired by the desire to tell off some idiot we know, or take a swipe at a political situation. Not being in favor of smoking in any sense of the word, I did a few anti-smoking poems early in my poeticizing. One was about Martians invading the earth and being so shocked at our bad judgment to smoke, they went home. The poems were clever and well rhymed, but hit the people involved, not the habit. I love a smoker as well as a non-smoker, so does the Lord, mothers, bosses, and everyone. It is **the habit** that turns up the temperature of those of us who don't smoke. I discarded the poems in question and several others I did afterward in which too much moralizing had crept in. I did a father/son poem long ago about a father teaching his son to drink with him as soon as he was of age, only to have the very habit turn out to

be responsible for taking his life. I ended the poem:

How that father has grieved
  over the life,
of a boy whose first "drop"
  was at nine.
Just to know he helped it go,
all by that one sip of wine.

Who would want to read that? There is plenty of moralizing, preaching, and fingerpointing in most amateur poetry. You have a right to go for a direct hit in some circumstances, but generally it is best to allow the reader to buy in as a bystander, not the target. For example, since I pay almost two million dollars in insurance premiums annually now, I wanted to take a swipe at those who cheat and lie in this arena, the false claim submitters and other leeches that bleed and impede the honest purpose of insurance. So I did it subtly and it did the job.

Why are insurance rates so high?
Last month they nearly robbed me!
Good thing I sneaked that windshield by
And that whiplash I got........probably.
          —DA 1971

I don't know the author of this next one, but I've always liked it. It gets the message over well to those who don't honor their medical bills. It puts God right in there on the "no pay" list, too...without moralizing or preaching.

When in trouble and not before
God and the doctor we adore
But when troubles are over
And things are righted
God is forgotten and
  the doctor is slighted.

Offering the reader choices and
suggestions sure beats beating on them
with "this is right and that is wrong."
Nothing wrong with having good strong
opinions in a poem, just read it over and
rewrite it if you have to so it isn't judgmental.

(Judgmental)
We have drugstore cowboys
  all over our towns
It sure is stupid to dress like
  those clowns.

(Opinion)
We have drugstore cowboys all over our
  towns
Maybe competition to our circus clowns.

I cast many of my poems into the "defang" (or avoid getting punched out) file,
but these two next ones I kept because I
believe all of us struggle with wanting
what we don't have and letting our "don't
haves" give us a second-rate life because
we think of it that way. I sat on a volcano
in Hawaii one day and whipped this one
out, making fun of we humans' ridiculous
coveting!

After writing three best-sellers on
getting rid of clutter, I felt maybe the
moralizing in the one on the following
page was justified:

The Grass is Greener in Prison

We are never satisfied, by heck,
because we always stretch our neck.
And that view of what another owns
puts green needles to our bones.
For what we have within our nooks
never measures up to how theirs looks.
Their food smells better drifting past,
their TV is clearer (without a mast).
He makes more money on the job,
his kids mind better than our Bob.
Their animal sheds no speck of hair,
and their sheets are cleaner hanging there.
That other husband is oh so kind,
and the wife is sexier all the time.
In drought, it still rains on their yard,
Its ground is soft, was never hard.
Their cars run better at any age,
their pictures appear in the lifestyle page.
Their plants are greener, so nursery fresh.

Their long vacations just seem to mesh.
They lounge in back, never tense,
no one is ever sick across that fence.
They inherit money in figures six,
and they can diet, just for kicks.
Their hair stays just the way it's combed.
And there isn't a restaurant they haven't
  roamed,
Their water tastes of the deepest wells.
and of chlorine it never smells.
Their stereo has a classic sound,
and no cockroach is ever seen around.
Their place never seems to need some
  paint,
and yes, the mother-in-law is a hallowed
  saint.
A waste of life is all this "covet stew,"
'cause they are thinking all this of you.
—DA 1986

Too Much

It's "enough" we need for life and
thrill
But it's never enough, so we
overkill.
More and more we have to nab
All choked and smothered and still
we grab.
Too much? Indeed it could be
Because of all those things "there"
for you and me.
There are too many channels—too
much pitch
And noise, and litter in every ditch.
There's too much food to select
and eat
And overpaid people dead on their
feet.
Too much published, too many
lawsuits
Too much ownership and too long
the commutes.
Overdoment in travel and in
freeways
Toys, condos, and
vacation days.
It's too
easy to
buy, too
easy to sell

Too much political wishing well.
Too many meetings and reports
Too much emotion spent on
sports.
Too many fingers ringed, to
measure wealth
Too many unworn clothes, too
much "restoring" health.
Too much rent and tax and
overpriced
Drugs and luxuries all overspiced.
Too much "gimmee," "mine," and
"more"
Too many bottom lines for keeping
score.
Too much stuff that fills the air
And too much drinking every-
where.
Too much taken from nature's
crust
Too many "deals" that embarrass
trust.
Statements of purpose are dotted
with "things"
While we sacrifice ever more for
these smothering flings.
Aw…promiscuity, swearing, just
too much stink
Isn't enough much less than we
think?

—DA Pittsburgh 5:30 am, October 1989

This last poem is a good reinforcement of what we should remember whenever we find ourselves starting to "moralize" in verse.

Reformation

Aren't we all reformers in
  our little hearts,
telling others when to
  stay and stop and start?

Knowing how, and wanting
  everything to fix
Government, schools, and
  even politics.

For society, the media, we have a better
  route.
We know just what to do, to straighten this
  world out.

Notice, though, our reforming is of the
  other guy.
Seldom do we start at home, with both you
  and I.

Clubs don't need reforming, nor need we
  retool groups
It's always **individuals** who constitute the
  troops!

—DA March 1997

"IN-HOUSE" POETRY
(for Associates and Friends)

If we did a survey, I'd bet that at least 75% of the poems most loved and enjoyed are "in-house" poems. This means poems, often humorous, written to be used and enjoyed within a certain circle (of friends, associates, or coworkers). Let me give you some examples here.

Several different businesses operate in my corporate office: a professional clean-

ing company (Varsity, Inc.), my publishing company (Marsh Creek Press), and a mail order company that sells cleaning supplies (The Cleaning Center). These are all in different parts of the building, but the kitchen and some central areas we share. As in your office, certain people's desks always offer certain goodies—the phone order computer room desk, for example, always has a big jar of long red licorice sticks. Any trip by is sure temptation. Once during a licorice attack I jaunted by the desk and the big bottle was empty! To make a contribution toward more and give the newest employee some spotlight, I left a twenty-dollar bill in the jar with this note.

If you wonder where all the Twizzlers went,
so fast they disappear!
Tis not by Marsh Creek Press they be spent,
nor the Varsity people dear.
The culprit lurks in the warehouse aisles,
the one we should subpoena
I traced the snitcher by the wrapper piles
Tis our red licorice lipped Tina!

That was **her** poem and she proudly showed it to everyone in the office. This type of thing is poetry's best use, in my opinion—much better, in this case, than just tossing in the money or replacing the candy.

Another of my poems highlighted another employee, Kathy, the head honcho of our mail order department (which sells cleaning supplies like Top Gloss wax). Kathy had calendared the due date of her new baby, but the day arrived and her new youngster didn't. As the days passed and it didn't arrive and didn't arrive, she was teased quite a bit by her husband Doug and boss Grant with jokes and puns relating to delivery (the mail, the freight, etc.) I chose to put my own comment on the situation in (you guessed it) a little ditty called "The Back Ordered Baby."

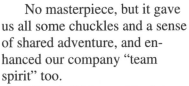

A myth? It was nine months ago, we
  thought it dilly dally
When a baby was back ordered by
  our famous Kathy Alley.
It began to grow, we didn't guess, a
  bite from a mosquito?
Or perhaps a little bulge from
  another lunch burrito?

Soon there was no doubt that the
  baby had been shipped,
But the arrival time came and went, that's what got us
  ripped.
The baby didn't show its face the day that it was due
So Kathy tried a thousand things, as inside it grew.

There she was at six A. M., stacking caddies like frozen
  cods,
And now we hear, loud and clear, Las Vegas is giving
  odds!
That unnerved the UPS and old Doug is really miffed
We now suspect she's saving it, for a Christmas gift.

She then slung cartons of rubber mats, twenty stories
  high—
we begged and cheered but that little rascal didn't try.
  It became apparent that little shipment now was boss.
  So Kathy tried a slicker move, she gargled in Top Gloss.

We punched all gestation programs on Grant's new Mac,
The answer came, "She's to blame; should we try the
  torture rack?"
Kathy used her week's vacation and still delivery wasn't
  made,
We are sure that when it comes it'll be in second grade.

Judging from the other kids, the waiting's worth it, so
we'll just call that Back Order Baby, little sweet B. O.

No masterpiece, but it gave us all some chuckles and a sense of shared adventure, and enhanced our company "team spirit" too.

I live in Idaho, cold winter country. It's dropped to thirty below for week at a time and there are months when the temperature is never above zero. Then for seven years my family and I moved up to the ski resort, Sun Valley, 6000 feet above sea level and colder. Many a winter I contracted to shovel seven feet of snowfall off the roofs of the condos and other buildings. One week my business was called to open an area in Boise, Idaho, about three hours driving time from Sun Valley. I was scheduled to go there with the manager-to-be, Rex Turner, and he was going to drive. The weather was clear and ice twinkling cold, thirty-five degrees below zero.

Having long ago learned the chances of perishing if stranded in a vehicle or in a wreck, I took my thirty-below down sleeping bag, my insulated coveralls, and other essentials. While we were enroute the truck drove perfectly, with just one hitch, a broken heater. It was slow death by freezing while riding. I did a Robert Service poem (not intentionally) called frostbite frolic. Here are a few verses of it to give you an idea of how cold it was and how I expressed my sentiments about the situation to our staff:

Frostbite Frolic

Shivers you'll have when you read this, turn on your
favorite burner,
for Dan McGrew was a heat lamp, compared to ol' Rex
Turner.

We had to travel to Boise, I agreed to answer Rex's
peals
But little I knew of the method, it was a '69 igloo on
wheels.

Impossible you say, it just couldn't possibly be right
Be careful when you read this—your eyeballs will get
frostbite.

The Chevy Van was like a fridge, frost hung on the
metal bare
It looked as if they could have filmed Dr. Zhivago there.

I knew that soon warm air would come if we were to
ever survive
I began to feel like a side of beef hung in a locker half
alive.

All the way to Shoshone my teeth did the saber dance
And my finger nubs scraping frost didn't have a chance.

Turner kept the defroster on and said with a confident
lick
"These blowers will keep the windows so cold no frost
could ever stick."

My coveralls were 20 below, that bag was 30 more
That made minus 50 I could stand, before I'd be frozen
to the core.

I know you won't believe this, but I swear that it is true
That before 18 miles were gone, the frost came creeping through.

What a way to go, I thought, frozen in a van
Right in with the buffer, mops, pads, and half used Ajax
cans.

—DA 1973

We laughed over this and will continue to laugh in the years to come.

I've been a scoutmaster for many years, and in-house or "custom" poetry works its magic equally well with young people. Once my troop and I were on a long trail hike at Camp Philmont in New Mexico. We would camp one night and then march ten or fifteen miles to a new camp the next day. The march was through the peaks of New Mexico and to add spice to the trail dust, I'd add a two-line rhyme to the 1, 2, 3, 4 Army march step:

Oh scouting is a heck of place
You have to look at Condie's
face
Sound off 1,2, Sound off count
3,4
Bring it back 1, 2, 3, 4—1, 2, 3, 4.

Now the next scout in line had to come up with a stanza and he knew it better be good. Most had laid awake half the night getting something to insult or rhyme. Finally the spindly little voice of a thirteen-year-old:

I hate to march
behind old Dan
His pack smells
like a garbage can
Sound off...(and
so on).

The next scout could hardly wait his turn, a chance to be heard in verse:

Our scoutmaster can't even read a map
The food he cooks tastes like crap.
Sound off…

The whole troop would cheer and laugh, and once through the line of twelve, I would take my turn again making some verse about one of their verses (much to my delight of my tenderfoot poets).

Well my cooking
   might lack
   some savor,
But I added
   Galyne's
shorts to give it flavor.

By the time we reached the last rounds no scout had time to make a verse ahead and had to do one on the spot, and they did, all of them. Some of them had never made words rhyme in their life and yet were chirping them out in unique cleverness.

Riding in the bus to attend a scout jamboree another time, I was with thirty-eight scouts and four leaders. I wrote a verse for each scout on the bus (to the tune of "Too Old to Cut the Mustard Anymore").

Now when ol' Shay Browning was young
   and in his prime,
He made it to chow in record time
But now he's old, and high school bound
He eats his food right off the ground.

This in memory of a recent incident in which this young man had dropped a donut and it rolled down a hill. He chased it and ate it, much to the moan of the troop.

Halfway through the trip the boys started retaliating with similar verses about the leaders and were they good! Now hear this—after this three-week trip, Niagara Falls, Big League ball game, the Rockettes (seventy wow legs), Gettysburg, Six Flags, roller coasters, $1200 apiece spent in ten days in the most astounding camp in the world, guess what they remembered best and wanted afterward… **a copy of the verse about them!** I tell you, people treasure verse that is tailored to the person or the situation. Anybody can write it and everyone will love the result, it's a real life enricher.

When you are writing "in-house poetry, you can have a lot of fun with innuendoes and allusions, things that your special audience will be well aware of, whether that audience is one person or a whole family or department. The poem that follows, for example, was written about a brilliant editor from the East, environmentally conscious to a fault. She does, however, have an even more dominant passion—cats, fourteen of them cavorting around her place. Mentioning this in the verse (which I sent with a red safety vest) enriched the poem a lot, because people love to be recognized for their eccentricities.

The Bag Lady

Upon the grades of Flat Run Road,
a figure lurched with a heavy load.

I drew close to see a K Mart bag
laden with cans in a bulging sag.

A wayfaring lass with desperate hands
was picking and mashing discarded cans.

To save the planet? Cash for cats?
Who knows? Perhaps to discourage rats!

Forlorn indeed, with heaving chest,
Could plain old exercise be her highway
quest?

As I passed, I must relate,
That woman edited my license plate!

Suspicion released, methinks it best
That she wear this Idaho highway vest.
—DA February 97

Jackie Luke, the wife of one of my cleaning company's major stockholders, Arlo Luke, is blessed with a great personality and character plus! In the early days of their marriage (and our company), she became famous for her noodles, which seemed to be the only thing she ever cooked and served. I wrote a poem once to playfully commemorate this, and the delightful gourmet cookery she eventually moved up to. Here is the first stanza:

There is nothing like having friends from the deep south. Their personalities and accents enrich we Northerners. Two of my friends, Dave, a business associate, and Kermit, a big, kind fellow, were characters indeed—every trip to see them was a once-in-a-lifetime experience. Here's a little verse I wrote in a humorous attempt to describe them:

Old Buddies

They eat raw oysters and
  horse trade guns
While their wives have
  nylons full of runs.
They've convinced each
  that they are winners
Excusing their faults as
  "Southern Sinners."

"Stay and eat with us, Don ol' pal," Arlo said to me,
"My new bride will cook some chow, just you wait and see."
Thus I heard pots and pans, raising a diligent noise,
It sounded like quite a feed Jackie was whipping up for the boys.
Two hours went by as she toiled away, finally announcing the serving date,
Then she dished up her only dish, rubber noodles on a plate.
The next 12 times I suppered there at the Lukes' fine residence,
Always we had noodles, by choice or coincidence.
Have you ever tasted Noodle Jello, or Noodle Chocolate Cake,
Or Noodle Pie, Noodle Soup, or maybe Noodle Steak?
Even on a picnic high in the primitive hills,
When her salad came forth, twas Noodles minced with Dill.
"Oh, Don," Jackie would say, from beside her tiny poodle,
"It seems ever time you visit us, we're always having noodles."
So for 13 years, noodles was the dish she produced so well,
Everything else she tried to cook even had a noodle smell.
And sometimes Arlo came to work singing "Yankee Doodle,"
I'd swear at times from a certain side he started looking like a noodle.
—DA 1973

Material for your in-house verse is everywhere—in meetings, letters, notes, deliveries, conversations, personalities, and daily, weekly, yearly, and once-in-a-lifetime happenings.

WORK Poems

No matter what kind of work we do, it needs some humor, humanitarianism, inspiration, and sometimes, some prodding. Good verse can be more effective than a strike or picket line. At least a third of my verse is work-related and much of what I've collected from others, laughed over, enjoyed, and re-read has its source in the workplace.

My own profession is cleaning and I tell you, folks, janitors are good poets. I've found verse hung (in disgust) on toilet seats, attached to paychecks, on vehicle steering wheels, closet doors, on desks, and on doors. I've been handed it in hallways and in meetings.

Putting a work situation in poetry gives you unlimited resources and potential. Need a change made? Put it in verse. A potentially explosive little situation in our office was corrected with this simple rhyme posted on a coworker's desk.

Sweet Thief

Who darkened the door of my office booth?
Surely a clue, they had a sweet tooth.
For in this desk I had twenty pairs
of my favorite snack, cinnamon bears.
I returned to savor them, hungry and lean
only to find that the platter was clean.
My tummy is growly, nobody cares,
Please return my cinnamon bears.
—DA 1992

The whole office chuckled, the thief was touched, and new bears appeared the next morning and never strayed again.

One of my cleaning company executives, manager of the California District and quite a poetic janitor, tired of cleaning the ever-reappearing mildew, etched this fine verse in a crop of it:

Mildew, mildew on the wall,
In the sink and down the hall,
You think it's gone? It comes creeping back,
In glowing blue, orange, and black.
How must I deal with this sporey villain
I fondly call, bathroom penicillin.
—Steve Gibson

In another poem, he expresses his love for his job:

In praise of the toilet

The toilet is a marvelous machine
A lofty sentinel surveying the scene.
The joy they bring,
these porcelain pedestals.
Much as I love to touch
and glean them.
I wish to heck
Someone else would clean them!
—Steve Gibson

To move now to the publishing workplace, the editor mentioned earlier often gives me cause to comment on her tireless quest for "more" in my literary efforts. This time I did it in verse:

She calls at midnight
with a list
of tidbits, leads, and
all we've missed.

"Do it, Donald!"
she seduces me
"the ones you like...
just two or three..."

Every morning, every day,
and into the night
Her erotic craving is
Write, write, write!
—DA March 1997

Perhaps I shouldn't include the crudest of my early poetry, but the poem you will read next had a definite purpose. The fact that I had the nerve to write it was one thing, but to send it to a major client, the Bell System, and have it copied and sent through the other telephone operations nationwide, was a little much. The Bell System at the time was the biggest single business entity in the world. The building we initially agreed to clean for them was the first ever done by a cleaning contractor, rather than their own in-house cleaning crew. We were extremely successful, and instrumental in the conversion of the entire Bell System nationally to contracting. We grew with them to cleaning thousands of their buildings in many states.

In the business of keeping a building full of delicate electronics clean, there were rules (no moisture, no fires, no dust, etc.) and they were rigid. And when something was wrong it wasn't "come in the morning," it was COME RIGHT NOW. We got such a call once and it seems the sewer that served the local Bell building (which had had problems a couple of times before) was getting old. That night a major backup occurred, and before long me and two top Bell executives from the area were down in the mess, protecting our national communications network. We finally freed the sewer clog after much effort and stress and when we were done we were thoroughly "pooped." I came home and before I showered and discarded my sewer shoes, wrote this little ode and left it, that night, on the manager's desk:

Sewer Sadness

By another sewer rat, Don Aslett

Oh, sewer fair, you punished us when your refuse returned on high,
For what the ladies flushed away, it seems you didn't buy,

Because of this, the foul filth already headed down,
Sought its way back up the pipe and on the floor was found.

Oh, Commercial got an inch or so of the social matter's calls,
And the landing going down the stairs resembled Niagara Falls.

The odious flow from up above, found its way into the ladies lounge,
It found no plug and soaked the rug—that nasty rampant scrounge.

Our hero, Butler, cried the alarm, sacrificing his finest shoes,
Baker and Hodge became all-day sewer rats trying to rid the silent ooze.

The culprit source we all did seek, of the pipe became the looters,
And soon was found a napkin bound, on the cable of the Rotor Rooter,

Now we don't criticize nature's plan whereby the ladies monthly suffer,
But it should be acknowledged that its second use is not a sewer stuffer.

—DA 1962

It must have worked—that was the last sewer backup for the next thirty years. Never underestimate the power of poetry.

After witnessing the popularity of this effort many poems to the Bell managers and staff, and my employees followed (a poet will resort to any means of getting their poems read!). We all got a laugh out of them and the job got done.

The Bell System was always building, always remodeling, and to a professional cleaner that meant constant dust, sawdust, wire clippings, and sheet rock sandings—even on the toilet seats. The trash bins were always so loaded with construction debris there was no place for our office waste. I had to climb up and tromp them down before we could fit anything in. It was miserable, and worse, those big construction brutes would help themselves to our cleaning supplies during the day, stealing our brooms and containers and when we arrived to work, nothing.... I did an "Ode to Bell Systems Building Construction," and let me excerpt a line or two from it:

The seventh wonder of
   the world is... will
   they ever stop
   construction in phone
   buildings, from bottom
   to the top,
Bolts and clippings and
   round cable reels
Leave damage marks
   like hot rod wheels.

It was a straightforward little ditty I posted on some supervisor's door. None of our equipment reappeared nor did the dust disappear, but I felt better!

Your job is a big part, often the biggest part of your life. If you learn to love it,

seldom is it "work," and I learned to love and appreciate the Bell System. What a dynamic, well run company. The people were loyal and rarely criticized their company and there was no jealousy among employees. It was a joy to work around them. Bell's price for phones and service was low and they operated more efficiently than any company in the world, beating other telephone companies by about 300% in all indexes. Like most businesses they had their own language for departments, parts, and positions, and gradually (since at least three quarters of our business at the time was contracting for them) we learned it. "Traffic" was the operators, "toll" was the across-country messages, "plant" was the office that housed the communications equipment, etc. But I soon discovered who it was that invented acronyms. It was for sure the Bell System. They could almost conduct an entire conversation in acronyms, and often some communication between them and us was lost in the "code." Although I had other Bell poems and essays (and even a handwritten thank-you from John DeButts, chairman of the board of Bell), I'll share my last thrust to them with you. By the way, everything Bell System lived and breathed by was in the Bell System Practice book, called the BSP.

BSA (Bell System Acronyms)

It took great efforts as a babe, to learn to da
   da and goo,
And I had to master other words, as into life
   I grew.

At last I gained all the words needed, to
   communicate and survive,
But then someone invented the acronym, a
   new language to derive.

From USA to PTA I learned, and could
finally even list 'em,
But I wasn't yet ready for the time I met,
the engineers from the ol' Bell System.

As I sat one day with two of them at a nice
clean luncheon table,
I heard this conversation, but to understand
it, I wasn't able.

"BEMARR should C & X our log when BER
P-Wacs."
"Yeah, the T.S.P. uses more B.O.E. to beat
the 6-10 sales tax."
"I'll have M&M check the H.V.A. at the 4A
south for me."
"Bell task 10M if it fails, blame it on ol' W.E."
"That ESS and PBX, L.P.A.'s boost to AT&T."
"We'll operate up to date with our brand
new BOCC."

Refrain:
Now there's a glorious place in heaven, pre-
wired just for you and me…
and there must be a formula of acronyms,
for how to get there…
Somewhere in the BSP.

The Seven Dwarfs whistled while they
worked, and you can give your job a "jab"
or two in verse, right while you're doing it!

Life's Effort Essays, or "PRODUCTIVITY POETRY"

Just about everyone these days is
seeking the secrets of being a number one
in life—there are books, classes, tapes, and
training sessions everywhere on how to be
"the best" for yourself or your company.

I teach seminars and write books on
this very subject, too, but I think poetry or
verse dealing with it could be more effective with less time and paper used. For
years now, whenever I've heard or experi-

enced stories of great accomplishment, I've
written not just essays and articles but
verse on them.

Dwight Eisenhower's personal chef,
for example, was a guy named Kiser Bell. I
was involved in a maintenance bid on a
hospital in Florida while Mr. Bell was
being invited to take a position there. In the
process, someone asked him for his
resume, and I heard his reply: "I don't have
a resume, I let my cooking do my talking."
That was a great line, so I sat in the lobby
and jotted this summary of his super
message for all we job seekers.

Works… Not Words

He stood before the
board, his merits
on review,
A quiet, humble kitchen chef, who sought a
job to do.
By age, stature, and experience, he could
easily qualify
But still they asked him, "Tell us, just how
well do you fry?"
He smiled and leaned toward the group,
His words were free of mocking,
"Sirs, I have no speech for you. I let my
cooking do the talking."
—DA 1979

Here is another little verse on a similar
theme:

Image
You may fool the world with cosmetic
disguises,
But what you produce, never lies
Many crow, but never show…
—DA September 1978

124

Though some acknowledgment may be given at times to the work involved, deep down, **many people think that high achievers are just plain lucky**. I heard two people in one day refer to individuals who had moved mountains in various areas as "having a golden touch." Boy, is that bull—I didn't want to debate them so I versed them.

The Golden Touch

Everything he
  touched turned to
  gold, so they say.
They are wrong, cause touching never
  piled up pay.
You have to grab, beat, wrestle, and
  pry;
handle opportunity like do or die.
You squeeze, you siege, you twist and
  tear,
a touch will never put you there.

—DA May 1986

We've all heard lectures about the importance of **perseverance** to accomplishment. Here is a verse that gets the point across even better. I wrote it because "finishing"—taking a project all the way to the end—is one of my own weaknesses. Often writing a poem about a problem or lack is a real step in the direction of fixing it.

We've all read essays or heard "sermons" or have opinions about sticking to the job for morality's sake. What about doing it for our own sake?

Finishing

Starting is easy, I tell you, Mister.
New and fresh always seems
  crisper.
Cause after a while it all gets so
  routine
and duties move in a much
  slower stream.
Manuscripts, meetings, and
  marriages for sure
become like clean up, straighten
  up, and lock the door.
The finishing, the final, evolves to
  a grind.
Competition is fierce for a share
  of your mind.
"Launch" gets the glory, first
  steps are full of reward,
But the journey and the tilling
  strike a different chord.
That final fitting and filling
  require a real risker,
Finishing is **tough**, I tell you,
  Sister!

—DA May 1995

Same Old Grind

A misuse of meaning, I do find
how we read the phrase "to grind."

Most will readily vote or judge
to rank it synonymous with "drudge."

To labor, toil, sweat, travail
a treadmill experience to weep and wail.

A winner views "grind" differently,
as a process perfecting you and me.

For grind removes excess and rust
hones a shine from ugly crust.

Grind **can** blunt if we face it flat
Wise angling, however, will prevent that.

Will "grind" point you up or pull you
 down—
are you a quitter or a craftsman sound?

To sharpen points and make edges
 clean
grind's a friend, who will make you
 keen.

—DA May 1997

bells with them. What they do is entirely their business, after all, but I did hear a wise man once say, "Ah retirement, there is just something not right about that word!"

To pacify myself on the matter as in many things when I have a message, I versed it. Here is one stanza out of the middle of the one-page poem:

When senior birds quit building nests
Their wings get full of lead.
Their beaks get dull and that's not all,
They lose feathers from their bed.
Would you like some breathing room
To gain some ground a while?
Remember there are no traffic jams
in the second mile.
—DA 1981

One day someone wistfully remarked that I was "always too busy for them." Giving to and helping other people has been the central theme of my life, and to be told such a thing during a time when I was donating in all directions by phone and mail, and my office was open to anyone in the world, was, well, irritating. (What it came down to was that this person felt that if I was doing anything else at all then they couldn't bother me or attempt to fit themselves into the schedule.)

All of us who want to get anything done learned long ago in life that sitting idly by, waiting around to have someone give you a call is not the most efficient method. Instead of tapping this fellow on

Things in my business one year were mounting to the height of complexity— there were minority, equality, and pollution lawsuits to be dealt with, complicated perks and health care planning for employees, and forty new competitors backed by big companies entering the market. Yet every day I seemed to get news of more of my classmates "retiring." I don't think our brain gets fully developed until we're sixty-five, and then we should have a good ten years more to really produce something. But my kidding my friends about still being youngsters and in their prime at fifty-five and fifty-eight, didn't ring any the side of the head and saying, "Wake up, friend, and jump into the battle with me, run alongside as I work and let's talk about or do your project," I sat down and versed it:

Too Busy

I'm available to talk or help,
But I won't be in camp like a
  sleeping whelp.
I'll be out in the trees, or down in
  the mine
at work on the job, in front of the
  line.
Opportunity doesn't snatch talent
  from the bench,
The people you want are out, in
  the trench.
"Too busy" is a virtue, not a vice,
You might even say it's
  accomplishment's price.
Reading news is a yawn—admit!
All life's merit is in **making** it.
Those minus a schedule
  tightly crammed
aren't awake enough to
  know they're damned.
A hand on the hoe doesn't
  eliminate me.
I'm never "too busy" and
  you know where I'll be.
  —DA Australia 1986

Let me end here with a verse that says a whole chapter's worth about effort and accomplishment, starting and finishing in just four little lines:

My soul, sit thou a patient looker-on;
Judge not the play before the play is
  done:
Her plot hath many changes; every day
Speaks a new scene; the last act crowns
  the play.
  —Francis Quarles

Poetry in Business

Poetry, that wonderful condenser!

Poetry—whether we are reading or writing it—has a built-in "squeezer." You haven't got pages or paragraphs to say it, only a few lines. If we had to communicate in business with poetry alone, I bet efficiency would go up 50% and paper clutter down at least as much.

I've read and listened to hundreds of articles, seminars, and talks on attitude, for example, the impact of positive and negative outlooks. Those writers and speakers go on forever, and generally get lost somewhere in their descriptions of positive and negative vibrations and the like.

Now read this simple little verse:

What one approves, another scorns,
and thus his nature each exposes.
Some see the rosebush full of thorns
Others see the thornbush full of roses.

It says it all, doesn't it?

We hear a lot about failures and downturns in the business world, yet the causes are often vague and they are vague because it is often little slippages that break big businesses down. My look at it through verse:

"Do," not "Did"

Foolish we, who gain the
    ground,
    Of friends and lovers, and
    customers sound.
We court and dine them from the start
To win them over, claim their heart.
Oh, how we work to get them there
Through kindness, duty, and even prayer.
But when we've got them at our side
We seem to always let them slide.
We set them comfortably at our rear
And treat them like some souvenir.
We're blind to their needs and deaf to their
    cries,
They're lost in our "later files," those guys.
As we coast "for granted" with weakened
    spine,
And never notice the slow decline.
Until they look for a brighter sky,
For always, fresh and better will peddle by.
So stupid! Their needs we overlooked,
They're gone! And now our goose is
    cooked.
If ignored through slight or skid,
Anyone will forget just what you "did."
It's "do" that counts and keeps alive
The spark, and helps love to thrive.
— DA Chicago, March 1991

Real Results

Salesman or order taker—which are you?
It makes a difference when there's a
    monster job to do.
For anyone can prosper and make most
    any sale.
When to the door, likely customers beat a
    trail.
Yes a smile is easy, as is being full of go
When clients seem to buy everything you
    show.
But when prospects are dimmer and the
    market has clear bounds
A mere order taker will never manage to
    turn things around.
A salesman is what we need when pickin's
    get slim
To spot and dig up customers, when the
    crowd is mighty thin.
The salesman will still profit when others
    whine or starve
He'll make new calls and always find new
    territory to carve.
While order takers nurse coffee and
    danish, crying out the blues.
To a double time schedule, the salesman
    always moves.
It's actually kind of easy to see which one
    you are,
Just tally up the sales you've made, in this
    month so far.

I spoke at a real estate convention once, and after my own presentation was through I listened to the other speakers and heard all the assembled Realtors brag or complain about "things out there." During one of the dull speeches, I attempted to summarize in verse the whole morning's speaking siege (including mine):

You can even create poetry when you're **sitting in a business meeting, taking notes** (those notes that are often jumbled and disjointed and never read, eventually tossed out). You can take notes in poems, which you will remember and re-read, and the process of writing them can help keep you from going to sleep.

At a university advisory meeting I

went to once, they were discussing the process and paperwork of selecting a new dean of the college. I jotted down my impressions of the prolonged procedural debates that followed in this little ditty:

Ha! Ha! Tis the day of documents
Too complex to absorb or find common sense.
A day we must leave such an audit trail
We can't even lift that paper bale.

A couple of other commentaries on paperwork I've made:

Forms = Faster?

These many forms that provide a space
To fill, report, or firm a case
Can be indeed be a clever tool,
But disaster in the hand of a fool.
Cause they don't manage or organize,
They don't digest or make you wise.
They don't inspire or measure you,
Nor sign or mail themselves, it's true.
They don't make summaries or do the work,
Although they can drive you berserk.

Their job is convenience—to display,
Record, compress information away.
They **are** indeed a helping hand
If done right the first time, understand?
But the quicker and better a job is done
the more forms we can shun.
— DA 1994

In Touch...with Not Much

In this race to communicate
"content" falls to second rate.
Phones, faxes, and Fed Ex
Instant transfer of a text.
We have contact at every turn.
For some **content** now I yearn.
— DA February 1997

In another meeting, I jotted this while a speaker droned on and on about "enhanced customer rapport and awareness."

Rah Rah

Signs and slogans, cheers and codes
About good service by the loads.
Standards posted all over the place
and mission statements in your face.
Oaths and promises, everywhere
About good manners and being fair.
Such noble verbiage makes me nervous
It foretells a decrease in
customer service.
— DA May 1996

Wouldn't it be interesting to see a big corporation conduct one of their meetings in verse? What if instead of producing pages of dry analysis and graphs, and getting back endless "executive" reports, the CEO said "Okay staff, we didn't meet our sales quota for July. At the next meeting you will bring your reason and solutions in a six-line poem." There would be lots of moaning and scrambling, but I'd wager everyone would come through with shorter, better, more pleasant to listen to, easier to understand presentations. They'd all be prouder of those presentations, too!

DEEP FEELING Poems

One of the best uses of poetry is to capture and comment on those "certain times" in our lives when something significant happens, good or bad. Acknowledging experiences like this with just a sigh or thanks is often not enough, especially for things we feel strongly. Recalling or reliving them later is not always so easy to do from just a memory alone. Combine the memory with a personal journal or diary entry, or better still, a verse of some kind. It doesn't have to be the best, pass any test, or even be published and copied for the rest of the crew in your life. It just has to help you to record the memorable events in your life, and how you felt about them. Some good things do happen only once, you may never see them again, so retaining the warmth and intensity of the experience is important. That one time is precious.

I captured the following images and impressions thirty years ago and can still feel and see them all as well as I did then.

The Best Thing I've Ever Smelled

Harvested grain and hay,
The drying, thawing ground on the first spring day,
Sagebrush, pine trees in the rain,
Metal being cut and welded and tempered for a gain.
A fresh baked loaf of pure whole wheat bread,
Plowed ground, sweaty horses, and a fresh clean made bed.

The Neatest Thing I've Ever Seen...

The baby calves turned loose into a large green pasture in early spring.
A four-year-old girl dressed up for Sunday School, in black shoes and lacy things.
An old burred pet dog at the school bus departure and return
And the parents of a child, a depot greeting, showing welcome and concern.

Now many years later, I have these poems to use and enrich my life. You can call poems like this "Deep Feeling Poems," "For Myself Poems," or anything you like, but you really must do some. They take so little time and last forever and then you don't have to hunt down and read someone else's, you have your own! Your own personal history is as great as America's or anyone in it, and your feelings are much more real because they are your own and you lived them... every minute.

We all have different things that strike those "very deep chords" in us. Consider the poem my editor did, for example, to record her feelings about a hard-won addition to her small farm in Southern Ohio:

Five Acre High

I'm five acres richer today
and for $10,000, what is my pay?
I no longer have to look over the line
and sneak across, and wish it were
    mine.
Don't have to look down at the deep
    quiet and dark
and wonder if it'll soon be a trailer
    park.
The little pond in the hollow full of
    peepers in spring
will not be invaded by a lot-maker's
    string.
Whatever's denned under the century-
    size sycamore,
Can go on sleeping, and even dare to
    snore.
The deer and wild turkeys and coveys
    of quail
will have a sanctuary that shall not fail.
The unknown creatures that make
    noises at night
From their mating grounds won't
    have to take flight.

I gain two osage oranges and an old
    walnut tree
and many a massive hickory.
A pawpaw, a willow, and moss-grown
    white oak
through whose tall branches the fox
    squirrels can poke.
A hilltop of young locusts, a secret cedar
    grove,
and plenty of fallen wood for the stove.
The rough-barked giants along the old
    fence
and a tangle of roses and briars, dense.
Thickets of honeysuckle and sassafras
No realtor or builder can ever harass.
An old filled-in well and some ancient
    apple trees
Wild grapes, blackberries, and raspber-
    ries.
Even a wet-season stream with a rocky
    bed
Forgive if all of this goes to my head!
                    —Carol Cartaino

What about this touching verse (in an interesting rhyme scheme) done by a mother to record the emotions of leaving "the nest" full of childhood memories behind forever now:

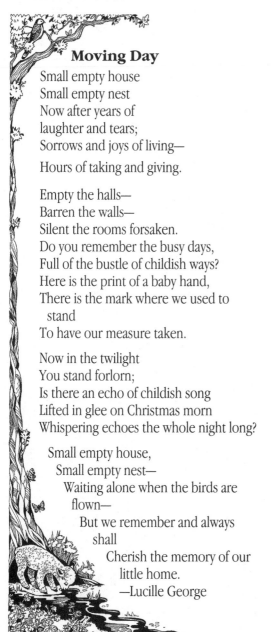

Moving Day

Small empty house
Small empty nest
Now after years of
laughter and tears;
Sorrows and joys of living—
Hours of taking and giving.

Empty the halls—
Barren the walls—
Silent the rooms forsaken.
Do you remember the busy days,
Full of the bustle of childish ways?
Here is the print of a baby hand,
There is the mark where we used to
 stand
To have our measure taken.

Now in the twilight
You stand forlorn;
Is there an echo of childish song
Lifted in glee on Christmas morn
Whispering echoes the whole night long?

Small empty house,
 Small empty nest—
  Waiting alone when the birds are
   flown—
   But we remember and always
    shall
    Cherish the memory of our
     little home.
      —Lucille George

Even if some of your first efforts to do a "deep feeling" poem come off as kind of silly or a little soupy, do it anyway.

I was driving home one day, for example, through forty miles of the countryside's best display of fall colors. It was one of those superb evenings when all the feelings of the past come rushing in and sentimentality takes over. I drove past fields where I'd labored with Dad and grandpas and cousins, past ponds where ducks and geese rose from the sound of the car, then blackbirds, and magpies from the fence posts—everything popped up in quick order as I slowed down to savor it a bit.

And then came the old house, the old abandoned homestead of my own family—engulfed in weeds, brown boards sagging, few windows left, but still proud and beautiful, making its last stand to testify of its long service to us.

I arrived home late and the family was asleep. I was too awake from the drive to go to bed and this was the first time I'd ever decided to write a deep feeling poem. I wanted to get what I'd viewed and felt down in something besides my journal that said "Drove from St. George to Idaho today in 5.5 hours, saw some nice scenery." I wrote the title OLD HOUSE (creative, huh?) down. I labored until about 3:00 A.M. and had what I thought was a masterpiece.

I went to bed on a high—capturing what I felt deeply in some (however imperfect) form gave me a shot of courage and peace and purpose. I think any link with the past does that. It was my first, and surely not my best effort. I asked my wife to read it, and reading it today, I know why she yawned as she read it. Here is an excerpt from it:

132

> Your eyes now sealed to dimming slits for
>   meditation's rest, your keen soul for all its
>   yield,
> How can the superficial verdict death
>   overlook dependence for your shield?
>
> Generations were measured in distance of
>   life, it took five of the living to equal your
>   years,
> You suffered the learning of wisdom 5
>   times, which saddened them not and
>   allowed you no tears.
>
> Seasonal treasures of all you partook, and
>   gleaned them as landmarks to your frame.
> For only the perspective survey of love can
>   harvest human affairs without a name.
>
> Your landscape still casts a wink of wisdom,
>   some bend from scars of work and play.
> Your creator's trees to defend your state,
>   aged, now hug you close to a promise it
>   will stay.

The whole poem was too deep, too complicated, like Milton's in a way. Especially when writing deep feeling poems, you need to beware of the #1 sin of beginning poets (see page 48)—trying too consciously to be poetic and profound.

Unless you saw and loved the house, this particular effort would go unappreciated, but I liked it and it did me a lot of good. And again, if that is all your verse does, that is one of the greatest values on this earth.

Poems to express LOSS and SORROW

Longfellow's famous line "Into every life some rain must fall" recognized one of the moments of living we all go through—times of loss, setback, sorrow, and sadness. This is a time of hurt and painful reality

when we generally feel helpless and alone—all of the idealism, comfort, and encouragement of friends cannot provide much relief. "Bearing it," the load or grind of grief is a deeply personal thing and it always makes us dig back into ourselves and find answers to questions we've ignored, like "Why am I here?" "Is it worth it?" "Why me?" and "What am I going to do?"

The natural extension of just thinking about all this is writing it down, notes or letters about it, mainly to yourself. There are more "sorrow" poems around than you imagine and they capture and express more than most "reformer" or "Beautiful day, isn't it?" poems ever do. Yes, using poetry in time of personal pain is of value, usually mainly to yourself. We could call these "release" poems. I wouldn't be too quick to share them with others but verses like this can be a good way to shed some sadness. They have a stronger shoulder than we do sometimes. Try it at your next time of trial.

Poetry for Funerals

The son of the Leo Bullock mentioned earlier is a good friend of mine. His name is Wayne and he is a gifted professional welder who has raised a beautiful family. One wintry February, he lost a little grandson, who lived for only a few days after birth. It was cold out in the cemetery when the service was held, with that little casket under the huge pine trees. Wayne, the grandfather, said a few words of comfort. He had stayed up into the night laboring to get his feelings down on paper and did so he did, in a verse of his own.

It fit, it touched, it was his and theirs and that is something verse can do and be—something you have a right to do with verse.

A sincere, well done verse by someone close to the deceased and/or their family will add something special to a memorial service. Or reading one of the departed's own favorite poems or better yet, one they wrote themselves. (Another reason to write your own poems—you will have a legacy of feelings to pass on.)

Putting an EXPERIENCE OR AN EVENT into a Rhyme

This is a good way to tell a story or an anecdote, as in the following examples.

The Brief Encounter

With blond hair flowing
With lips so sweet
You were the one
I just had to meet.
Then you smiled
With your teeth so rotten
You were the one
That was soon forgotten!

—James Yoakem

Experience poems are best and most easily done if drafted and completed as soon as possible after the event. Try to at least jot down or outline the most memorable circumstances or details right on the spot or at the scene.

Poems that TELL A STORY

The best long poems are story poems, however this doesn't mean even a story poem can go on forever. Poetry takes a little more energy to focus on and digest than other written forms. If you are telling a long story, keep it narrative, a story—don't get intellectual and complicate it with big words and over-poetic phrases. Read some of Robert Service's long narrative poems to see what I mean—pure simplicity. They move along and you understand perfectly what's going on all the time. Remember, too, that in a poem (just as in a short story, song, or book) you cannot fit in too many characters. A poem's virtue is in its message, not the size of the cast!

Don't be afraid on these longer story poems to let stanzas pour out in any order. When you get several of pages full you can

Water Skiing

The boat's out in the water
I'm floating in the lake.
By now I'm having second thoughts,
This is a big mistake.
The driver has the motor racing
And the rope is pulled real tight.
My skis are primed and ready,
And I pull with all my might.
Now my heart is pounding
As I get into my stance.
I'm glad I'm wet all over

Cause I just wet my pants!
I'm drug across the water
At a very frightful pace.
The wind is blowing in my hair
And water in my face.
Just when I'm getting tired
My legs feel like a rock,
The driver makes a stupid move
And runs into the dock!!

—James Yoakem

cut them up in sections and structure them into an order or flow.

RHYMING to MUSIC

You don't have to write the tune or even originate the lyrics, either. One of the most effective and enjoyable ways to entertain a group, large or small—any audience—is to take a popular song and alter the lyrics a bit, tailor them to fit the specific event or circumstances at hand. Is this plagiarism or violation of copyright? If you're doing this just for fun around the family circle, I doubt it. It's when you go more public with something like this, use it in a class or sell or market the result in any way, that you will have to be careful exactly what you use and how. When it comes to music, there are plenty of old favorites around that have been around so long they're "in the public domain"— available for anyone to use for anything.

Earlier I mentioned the idea of rewording nursery rhymes or other well-known old poems. Doing this with a song is even better. Of course you are going to get a personal example or two now (I'd love to hear yours).

After twenty years of cleaning people's houses I received many requests for lectures, workshops, and seminars on the professional way to clean. So I developed a pretty dramatic three-hour "cleaning show" and before you know it I was presenting it all over the country. I remember once traveling to the little town of Hooper, Utah, to deliver this presentation. About five hundred people came and instead of the host walking onstage and reading the usual two-minute introduction I supply the sponsoring organization with, four women dressed in "exaggerated housework attire" bounced onstage carrying a chair. A piano

tinkled out with the start of the famous song, "Mr. Sandman, Send Me a Dream," and wow! could those four sing, in perfect harmony, as good as the Platters sang the original:

Mr. Aslett, teach me to clean.
Bring down the cobwebs
Make my windows gleam.
Teach me your tricks
So I'll enjoy it.
But can I like to clean a dirty toilet?
Aslett, I'm a mess,
It's bound to ruin my happiness
So please come on and do your thing.
Mr. Aslett, teach me to clean!
—Camille Meyers

On the second verse they called me and sat me in the chair and continued to sing sitting on my lap, circling around me, etc. The word got out that this was a wonderful way to introduce the speaker, and so at many of the workshops I did for years thereafter there was an opening performance of this type (often done so well that they upstaged me!)

I just thumbed through my file and here are some examples of what followed:

"I've Been Doing All the Housework" (to the tune of "I've Been Working on the Railroad"). Grady Allen did that one. In

Alberta, Canada, they did "I'd Like to Teach the World to Clean" (and you can guess what tune that was sung to). You've probably heard the "Queen of the House" version of "King of the Road"—that made an appearance, too. I've heard Gene Autry's old theme song "Back in the Saddle Again" turned into "Back in the Restroom Again," "Tiptoe through the Waxed Hallway" emerge from "Tiptoe Through the Tulips," and Willie Nelson's "Mamas, Don't Let Your Babies Grow up to Be Cowboys" changed to "cleaners." All of these and many more were downright hilarious. People like the old tunes, and sit in anticipation of how the lyrics will be transformed. No matter where I went, or what kind of a place it was, Hollywood or Havre, Montana, these "takeoff" songs were all a hit. People everywhere could do it, and what's more, they really enjoyed it, at least as much as the listeners did.

We've all done this sometime. Do it more! "Custom songs" can add a lot to any occasion.

Having fun with SHORT VERSE

Your own, that is! Even in those expensive cards, where every word is well chosen and well edited, few people read every word of the long poems. You probably don't either before you send them off!

Let me give a couple of examples of how short verse can work for you.

A friend of mine who lives across the valley retired a few years ago, and we see each other only occasionally and briefly now. One morning I realized it was his birthday so I quickly packed up one of my company's nice uniform shirts (people kill to get them) with a four-line verse. His wife saw me a few days later and said, "He liked the shirt, but loved the note." A gift will usually take second place to a nice verse or note, so don't strain yourself or your pocketbook trying to find the ultimate gift. Concentrate on making the verse great and you'll come out a winner every time.

A couple of summers ago, "The Fourth" arrived again as it does every year and the highways and stores were madhouses. People were heading for the hills or the beach or the picnic grounds, hollering, drinking, eating, shooting off sixty bucks worth of bootleg fireworks, or traveling to the "big show" in town. As I contemplated all this running around and wild partying and spending, I realized how few of us devote a day like this to any truly personal time with our mates or families. So I decided to stay home with my wife, just the two of us. Instead of a watermelon or skyrockets, I brought home a dozen roses tied with a red, white, and blue ribbon. She was elated, but most of all by the verse I tucked in the roses:

> Why should I this Fourth of July roam
> When I've had forty years of the best
>   fireworks in the world
> Right here at home!"

Corny, but she liked it—and the red, white, and blue hearts I drew for a border.

Consider this short poem. It condenses about a chapter and a half of the average "child psychology" book down to two lines:

Bribes
The bribe you use to keep kids true
Will ultimately be loved more than you.
—DA May 1995

136

What about this six-word summary of a favorite snack from my "author unknown" file:

Brownies

Smack my lips!
Expand my hips!

Here's a couple more "shorties" on one of my favorite themes—accomplishment!

What else is there to do
If not pursue, pursue, pursue?
—DA 1985

The Counters

When all is said and done
More is said than done.
The "rah rah's" don't count for
much at all
The only thing measured is the run.
—DA October 1996

Less demanded, less expected
Less required, less accepted.
—DA October 1996

Once you try doing short poems, you can and will do more of them. Especially as those little situations crop up where they are really effective.

EPIGRAMS

There are poems or verses often called epigrams (or maybe better yet, little jabs) that are short and sweet. Maybe not always sweet, but they say much. For example, I worked for years on essays and lectures about chewing gum (a foul habit to most

well mannered people) and eventually found this my mind's summary of it.

I'll bred,
enough said.

Same with those who file fingernails in public, comb their hair, apply makeup, etc. My summary in short verse…

Public manicurist
is an impolite purist.

Here's a little household commentary in concise verse:

The Ridiculous Rescue

Shelved 20 years that
ugly jar
No value had passed
through it.
But when it finally falls from the bar
We break our necks to glue it!
—DA November 1997

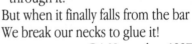

When writing epigrams, it may help to make yourself summarize the thought or situation you want to write about in not more than two sentences, or "twenty-five words or less." This will force you to "boil it down" to the essence. Then take what comes forth and see if you can convert it to rhyme with a witty twist.

TRAVEL POETRY

Let's jump to a subject we can all write about in some way—travel.

When reviewing possible poems to put in this book, I was surprised at how many poems I 'd written on travel—a lot! I was even more surprised when Carol, the editor who has edited all thirty of my books, pointed out that most of my travel verses were **negative**! It seems I have an attitude problem about travel.

At first I did write things like:

By the Glacier in Alaska

The light, the breeze,
the smell, in life at
last a pleasant lull,
The water's mist, pine
dew kissed, and
distant squeak of an
arguing gull.

As I traveled more and more, and travel began to punish instead of uplift me, my writing about it followed the same pattern. I guess I've traveled so much in the past twenty years that travel has become a "have-to" for me, rather than a delight and pleasure. I should be appreciative of the chance to fly all over the world and stay in gorgeous hotels and resorts and be picked up in limos, but I'd rather pitch manure in the horse corral now. I'm always so beat from it, the hours and hours of traveling and performing, that the cemeteries I pass almost look inviting. The most positive thing I can find to say about travel is that it offers me a lot of time to jot verses, while waiting, touring, riding, and filling the time in hotels and motels.

Let's take a look at a few travel verses now. After I'd traveled to a particular destination in my own car, on a train, and flying, I had to go back on a bus once. It was late and as the riders in filed onto the bus it looked like we were loading the cast of the Grapes of Wrath. I summed it up with this poem:

The Bus Ride

You Greyhound transport, curse your hide
You stop in towns where ghosts abide.
Your tinted transparent flanks display
Man's full struggle from dust to clay.
The schedule clock on the kennel wall
Can always lie to its transient haul.
May you lope forever through sleet and fog
Without my frame, you miserable dawg.
—DA 1974

The manners you encounter traveling can really get to you if you let them, and I do. Loud and aggressive crowds can stimulate some critical (if not obnoxious) verses. My apologies to the city in question, but I wrote it in this next poem like I've seen it—over and over.

Seeking the Like Level

I walked all through an airport
In a thoroughly Western town,
And noticed that throughout the place
There were weirdos walking around.
Necklaced men, uncouth in speech,
Women gaudily clad,
Throwing garbage on the floor
Treating people bad.
Soon they all seemed to funnel to one gate
Each other they had found,
They became a homeward group
All Miami bound.
—DA 1979

I don't know if there is anything that can heal a person after a long stay or even a fast trip to New York. After living on a ranch in the mountains of Idaho, then traveling five hours on a plane to get there, being in the depth of that city is like going from heaven to hell. There are lots of good people there, it is just mystifying how they can live so packed together and how all the toilets can flush. You just cannot tell people how it is there. Here is one attempt I made to do so:

An Extremely Prejudiced Poem About Cities

Now "town" I can tolerate
Having been raised on a farm.
It is a break from the hot sun's bake
A "village" definitely has its charm.
A "town" has movies and ice-cream stands,
That new clothes smell, and park lawn
   bands.

But now that I'm older and business bound
In big cities I am often found.
A visit there is a sinner's fate,
A place quite opposite from heaven's gate.

There are stray cats and dogs, thin and lost,
Birds with feathers stained from exhaust.
Spit on sidewalks, asphalt grime,
All kinds of drugs and crime.

City sirens, city slums,
City tyrants, city bums.
Tunnels, trams, and factory smog,
They call that poison "city fog."

We move each day past graffitied walls
Through crowds and traffic, and garbage
   hauls.
Generally beside a sludge-filled river
A dip in which would
   ruin one's liver.

Oh sure those "gor-
   geous" skylines bring
   me smiles.
When my distance from
   them is **twenty miles**.
      —DA October 1997

As the noise, irritations, lines and broken schedules multiplied, my travel writing evolved to:

Trip Report

How was my trip to Philly PA?
A perfect way to ruin a good day.

I sat by three sniffers who snorted and
   coughed,
Clutter dropped on my head, out of the loft.

Four noisy laptops surrounded me
Two coffee drinkers to slurp, sip, and pee.

Others were thrashing with newspapers,
   rattling sacks,
taking all the room with overstuffed packs.

Phone conversations just inches away
Bad weather and fog consumed my day.

Late and wait and no dinner plate
Crowding and climbing at every flight gate.

Cramped in a space designed for a midget
Next to forty-two smokers with horse
   breath and fidget.

The traffic to town was like a road parking
   lot
No use in complaining—the ticket I bought!
      —DA February 1997

Finally some of my verse started showing a little desperation. One should never become immune to the thrill of going and seeing and experiencing, but what they say about hotel rooms and rubber banquet chicken is so, and it can get to you after a while:

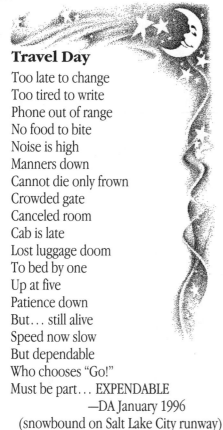

Travel Day

Too late to change
Too tired to write
Phone out of range
No food to bite
Noise is high
Manners down
Cannot die only frown
Crowded gate
Canceled room
Cab is late
Lost luggage doom
To bed by one
Up at five
Patience down
But… still alive
Speed now slow
But dependable
Who chooses "Go!"
Must be part… EXPENDABLE
—DA January 1996
(snowbound on Salt Lake City runway)

Now those of you who like or want to travel need to balance out my one-sided view. How about a verse on your next trip? Is this an assignment? No, a chance to maybe find out something about the world and yourself as I did. Send me one—I'll do another poetry book, this time mostly YOUR poems.

Rhyme of the Sexes

I've never written many poems (any, for that matter) about men in general. But women, they deserve more than poetry. They possess about 90% of the wisdom, the instinct, the sensibility, the spirituality,

and maintenance talent on earth. I dug out my very first poem on women. It rings a bit of "youthful gallantry," but proclaims the truth of feminine ownership of the world.

Women

We can scoff at the poetry they have inspired,
Ignore all the cannons they have caused fired.

We could shun all the kingdoms they've clearly won,
And disregard all the books they've managed to sum.

We can make light of the parts in history they've played,
Not take into account their teachings that have stayed.

We can minimize their worth in the birth of a child,
and not recognize discoveries or records they've filed.

All this we could do while away from their charms,
And know just the opposite while held in their arms.
—DA 1963

One day, attempting to sum up the "great women" in my life (at that time, maybe a combination of my two great-grandmothers, my mother, my wife, and maybe a dash of Sophia Loren or Julie Andrews), I jotted down this verse:

The Perfect Lady

By what mystique do you manage
to capture the thoughts of those around you?
Your marriage of grace and efficiency?

Your charm for all you see?
Your perfect face,
Your lips of lace?
Your anger suppressed,
Your zest undressed?
Can I love you?
You demand it.

I have others, and I'm sure you do too. Most of us have written and saved in "the file" somewhere things to be quietly (or secretly) read and savored. I found one poem in there I'd forgotten about that had quite a message. I went to an important publisher's dinner once with a sober group of executives. Everyone was going to that dinner with some sort of objective in mind for the negotiation—a percentage, a position, a compromise. But leave it to one of the more talented ladies there (who usually relied mainly on mind power to move people) to mount a surprise attack that turned the tide in her favor. Chuckling about it later, I knocked out this little verse that sums up the dinner well.

Objective

Nothing more amazes me
Than women's use of wardrobe weaponry.

For when she's decided she will impress
It's all science, not a guess.

No battle is as carefully mapped.
Meticulously is that body wrapped.

It's fashion strategy by coordinate,
As she robes to direct intended fate.

With the closet arsenal of the day—
a body draped a certain way.

Color? Cleavage? You can't assess
What a wanting woman does with a dress.
—DA September 1983

Turning to the members of the opposite sex now, it's my considered opinion that all too many of them are still caught up in modern-day macho-ism. The following are a couple of my poetic swipes at same.

"Man Club"

Poems are **not** sissy, so all you macho guys
Don't panic as you read this, or heave out
   some sighs.
For a friend you'll find poetry a pretty solid
   pick
Giving much more rush than a quick karate
   kick.
What we learn here of love and life and
   others' views of tender
Can work miracles, on our rough-cut
   gender.
—DA June 1997

Men's Macho Machines

A movie star? A fancy car? To be a
builder or composer?
More than this, or a lissome miss, most
men want a dozer.

It must be a king, or a power thing, to
own such a giant digger
The ultimate goal of so many is, to
possess one (or so they figger).

Don't take me wrong, in this song, of
masculine acquisition.
Subconsciously, it may be, that men
assume this earth moving mission.

Is it the noise, the joys of grinding
tracks that raise one's manly measure?
That huge blade, the change of grade,
or maybe greed and pleasure?

Such a macho buy, oh how they cry, for
a deal over twenty grand.

Then it borrows stares and waits for repairs—it fondles little land.

Those who can't close a deal of such enormous factor
Get a 4X4, or what's more, a useless garden tractor.

Lower on the chain of fame, and of power "neighbor show-ers,"
The average guy, will always buy, a bright red riding mower.

The real earth most men have to move is little indeed—
a shovel and a little sweat, is all they really need.

—DA July 1997

I'm afraid that some of your best "rhyme of the sexes" will come in moments of disgust or outrage at being pushed aside, forgotten, or taken advantage of. Often the culprit(s) you are writing about will really deserve the pointedness of your pen. But do read any such verse twice and keep it several days, then read it again before posting it.

A Big Howdy: COWBOY POETRY

"Wherefore art thou, Romeo?" might be more to some people's taste than "Where the Sam Hill ya bin, Slim?" But the test of time for poetry is how well understood and appreciated it is, and by how many.

I live out west in the middle of a movement called "Cowboy poetry," which is basically the process of polishing up some western folk yarns and setting them to rhyme. People of all ages and nations are irresistibly attracted to the American West and its culture—it has an appeal that includes "em" all. I travel the popular entertainment circuit quite a bit, and I often see these days a new feature in the programs of conventions and seminars. Where once a polished speaker or professional entertainer would have appeared, a rough, but "in charge" old cowboy or cowgirl walks up to the podium to read a down-home version of poetry that is easy to understand and all ages enjoy it. What it may miss by way of meter it makes up for with simple charm and realism.

Not long ago I was keynote speaker at a high school convention of eight hundred young people, ages fifteen to eighteen. It was a truly tough group to hold the attention of—they were good kids, but out of town and in a big hotel, and they were charged with energy. Experienced in things like this, I knew you had to either be the best or be ignored. Just before me, a 93-year-old woman in western dress hobbled up to the speaker's stand. I thought, "Poor thing, those young rowdies are going to eat her alive." Wrong! This lady was unquestionably the toughest act to follow in the more than 5,000 speeches I've delivered. She was masterful and both hypnotized those kids and cracked them up. What did she do? Recite some cowboy poetry. There was a poem about catching a pig, another about an outhouse, and another about someone seeing a washing machine for the first time. It was all GOOD poetry, you and me poetry.

So just for the heck of it, if you've heard a yarn from "the folks" or know a great down-home story, sit down the next time you get a breather and write it up in the form of poetry.

142

Poems contain many great lessons of life

Ever picked up a line and used it in your life and discovered its source to be.... a poem? Poems contain many of the great lessons of life, that have steered and even saved lives over the years. I've heard at least a hundred people (to sum up some past regretted event) quote, "the saddest words of tongue and pen are the words, it might have been." This quote is so beautiful and its teaching so powerful, I'd like to have you read the whole poem. You'll like it so well, you'll read it to others. John Greenleaf Whittier wrote it, and it's called "Maud Muller."

Maud Muller

Maud Muller on a summer's day
Raked the meadow sweet with hay.

Beneath her torn hat glowed the wealth
Of simple beauty and rustic health.

Singing, she wrought, and her merry glee
The mock-bird echoed from his tree.

But when she glanced to the far-off town,
White from its hill-slope looking down,

The sweet song died, and a vague unrest
And a nameless longing filled her breast—

A wish that she hardly dared to own,
For something better than she had known.

The Judge rode slowly down the lane,
Smoothing his horse's chestnut mane.

He drew his bridle in the shade
Of the apple-trees, to greet the maid,

And asked a draught from the spring that
flowed
Through the meadow across the road.

She stooped where the cool spring bubbled
up,
And filled for him her small tin cup,

And blushed as she gave it, looking down
On her feet so bare, and her tattered gown.

"Thanks!" said the Judge; "a sweeter
draught
From a fairer hand was never quaffed."

He spoke of the grass and flowers and trees,
Of the singing birds and the humming bees;

Then talked of the haying, and wondered
whether
The cloud in the west would bring foul
weather.

And Maud forgot her brier-torn gown,
And her graceful ankles bare and brown;

And listened, while a pleased surprise
Looked from her long-lashed hazel eyes.

At last, like one who for delay
Seeks a vain excuse, he rode away.

Maud Muller looked and sighed: "Ah me!
That I the Judge's bride might be!

"He would dress me up in silks so fine,
And praise and toast me at his wine.

My father should wear a broadcloth coat;
My brother should sail a painted boat.

I'd dress my mother so grand and gay,
And the baby should have a new toy each
day.

And I'd feed the hungry and clothe the
poor,
And all should bless me who left our door."

The Judge looked back as he climbed the
hill,
And saw Maud Muller standing still.

"A form more fair, a face more sweet,
Ne'er hath it been my lot to meet.

"And her modest answer and graceful air
Show her wise and good as she is fair.

"Would she were mine, and I to-day
Like her, a harvester of hay;

"No doubtful balance of rights and wrongs,
Nor weary lawyers with endless tongues,

But low of cattle and song of birds,
And health and quiet and loving words."

But he thought of his sisters, proud and
  cold,
And his mother, vain of her rank and gold.

So, closing his heart, the Judge rode on,
And Maud was left in the field alone.

But the lawyers smiled that afternoon
When he hummed in court an old love-
  tune;

And the young girl mused beside the well
Till the rain on the unraked clover fell.

He wedded a wife of richest dower,
Who lived for fashion, as he for power.

Yet oft, in his marble hearth's bright glow,
He watched a picture come and go;

And sweet Maud Muller's hazel eyes
Looked out in their innocent surprise.

Oft, when the wine in his glass was red,
He longed for the wayside well instead;

And closed his eyes on his garnished rooms
To dream of meadows and clover-blooms.

And the proud man sighed, with a secret
  pain,
"Ah, that I were free again!

"Free as when I rode that day,

Where the barefoot maiden raked her hay."

She wedded a man unlearned and poor,
And many children played round her door.

But care and sorrow, and childbirth pain,
Left their traces on heart and brain.

And oft, when the summer sun shone hot
On the new-mown hay in the meadow lot,

And she heard the little spring brook fall
Over the roadside, through the wall,

In the shade of the apple-tree again
She saw a rider draw his rein;

And, gazing down with timid grace,
She felt his pleased eyes read her face.

Sometimes her narrow kitchen walls
Stretched away into stately halls;

The weary wheel to a spinet turned,
The tallow candle an astral burned,

And for him who sat by the chimney lug,
Dozing and grumbling o'er pipe and mug,

A manly form at her side she saw,
And joy was duty and love was law.

Then she took up her burden of life again,
Saying only, "it might have been."

Alas for maiden, alas for Judge,
For rich repiner and household drudge!

God pity them both! and pity us all
Who vainly the dreams of youth recall.

For of all sad words of tongue or pen,
The saddest are these: "It might have been!"

Ah, well! for us all some sweet hope lies
Deeply buried from human eyes;

And, in the hereafter, angels may
Roll the stone from its grave away!
                    —John Greenleaf Whittier

TEACHING and "BUILDING" WITH POETRY

Many people think of poetry as flowery, soft, and gentle—all in all a weak, romantic product. Yet if you look at its ability to influence and strengthen lives, you can easily see poetry and tough and firm. Poetry is more often **powerful** than gentle.

Just look at the effect on behavior and life conduct many poems have had. Poetry has certainly had a tremendous influence on my own life.

It's amazing how poetry can and will help us assimilate a moral or guiding principle. We quickly forget even the best-presented sermon or lesson, but put the same message in a poem, with the right rhyme and wording, and we hear it just once, and not only have it memorized but incorporated into our thinking and actions.

I remember as a very young man hearing someone talking on the matter of finding a girl or woman to date and someday marry. You wanted someone who was genuinely nice and good and kind, he said, and how important that was in the long run for a quality life. Pretty faces and curves and contours of body build often prevented or interfered with good sense and selection here, and so we end up with a bummer of a life. He said in summary:

Beauties in vain their
pretty eyes may roll
Sight strikes the mind, but
merit wins the soul.

That always helped me to look past fetching clothes, charm, and sensuality, and to consider people for their merit, not their makeup.

Poems Can Raise—and Answer— Some Important Questions

As a parent, employer, youth counselor, seminar leader, and person who has often held positions of leadership and authority, I've long been intrigued with the "molds" out there, the cause or the causes of things. Ever notice how society, the schools, teachers, parents, God, everyone gets the bad rap, when and if we discover we have a bad characteristic of some kind?

The word "handicap," for example, is one we hear a lot today. One day I found myself wondering where some handicap comes from, and I jotted it down.

Handicap

"SAD" we say when our eyes
observe
one handicapped from birth.
A crooked spine or useless limb
might label cruel this earth.
But sadder indeed, are we "fortu-
nate" ones
content upon a shelf,
We have no excuse, or reason for
disuse
because we deformed ourselves
—DA Honolulu 1981

At a Scout Jamboree once in Virginia, within one hour I heard blame heaped on "they"(for jobs not done, problems at hand, disappointments) more than seventy-five times. So I decided to take a look at this "they" in verse.

They

In a bind and going gray?
We start our search to find a "they"
Someone to blame, someone to pay
Always somewhere we seek a "they."
To take our problems, we even pray
For above and beyond, for an angel "they."
And for a spot our sins to lay,
We hope faith will produce a "they."
Caught, discouraged, in dismay,
For rescue we await that "they"
In all our efforts to find a way
We must face this truth: there is no "they."
If you do find a "they," that slippery cuss
When unveiled, that "they" is "us."
—DA 1993

We often see people—including ourselves—gnawing away at themselves over some past sin or setback, some decision or action of long ago. This was my attempt to put this particular bad habit in perspective.

Past Present Future

So maybe you don't like what happened
What you were and did back then.
And every inner evaluation
Places you far short of "Ten."
It's dead, it's past, and will never change.
Why let it torment your today?
Those old, bad sparks you fan to life
Can smoke and burn you away.
You alone determine your worth
No one is researching you.
No appraisal of past status
Can outline what is now you.

There is no room for future flight
In souls who fight the past.
Put it behind you, and you will find
Forgiveness heals us fast.
—DA August 1997

In a similar vein, here is a verse focusing on how few events or circumstances in our lives are truly accidental.

Fault

We choose where we cruise
and select where we bruise.
We write all our news
About win or lose.
We locate our status quo
By the direction we decide to go.
—DA August 1997

How often do we have an unexpected loss—of position, cash, character, client, or headway, and then we ask ourselves WHY? The answer is often "slippage," and here is an excerpt from a poem on that subject.

Slippage

What gnaws and needles and kicks us around
more than that ugly action of LOSING GROUND.
Struggling long a goal to crack
then losing your grip and slipping right back.
Setting a standard! Conquering firm!
Only to retreat in a shameful squirm.
Yes sacrifice! Accomplish a mission.
But weaken somewhere, and lose that position.
To vow with valor, free yourself from a curse
only to trip, and suffer a reverse.

A temper controlled! A lust put away.
Why triumph never enjoyed such a day.
But slippage creeps in after all of that fight
and topples you from that envied height.

146

Seeing all the attention an unfortunate animal (finally) got one day reminded me how often it seems to take disaster to get action out of us. So I poemed it:

For the Soul of a Dead Horse

A horse so fine escaped its pen,
  and after wand'ring the black-
top
The highway center line it chose,
  as its place to stop.

This verse might have ended
  here, if any passerby
had reported or corralled the
  roaming steed behind a fence so
high.

But every driver was "too
  pushed," so the horse just stood
his road
and honking horns and
  skidmarks soon advertised his
abode.

For three days and three nights
  every traveler had no time
and so the animal stood his
  ground, on the yellow line.

It had to happen... and finally
  did, on the third dark, dreary
night.
A "too late!" screech and a
  thud—the horse was not all
right.

Now that the noble steed was
  dead, interest was aroused,
and in minutes eleven cars the
  accident scene now housed.

All the neighbors who heard the
  brakes hurried to the spot
to help the sheriff and spout "I
told you so's" about the horse
who now was not.

Among them were many who'd
  dodged the subject of remorse
Now stopped to show some
  interest in their neighbor's poor
dead horse.

They eagerly crowded around the
  corpse, saying "Tisk, so sad is
death."
Forgetting their total indiffer-
  ence when the noble steed drew
breath.

A big cattle truck arrived with a
  winch of strongest force
And with the help of seven men
  loaded on the broken body of
the horse.

All showed concern and mourn-
  ing for that stone cold steed
and for the pain and costs, the
  results, of this accidental deed.

What time and energy we give a
  dead horse, tis so very tender,
Yet we had no time or interest
  while he ran in all his splendor.

Let's learn a lesson from this
  horse who in greener pastures
lopes.
More care and time to living
  things might save us a world of
dopes.

—DA 1977

This next poem highlights our habit of viewing the actions of others with a jaundiced eye, an eye we rarely turn upon...ourselves.

An Ant

Twas always the other guy I read about
who fought the traffic, with honk and
    shout.
Who crowded for space on tram or train
Dashing for cover from a Wall Street rain.
Who thrashed in the commerce and
    business world
with a new briefcase and a tie clip pearled.
Practicing and prancing the ethics of callous
Am I in Salt Lake or in Dallas?
Measuring meetings, investing the pay
gaining, gaining, he hopes every day!
Tromping old ladies with street politics,
scurrying on board with line-breaking tricks.
Un-chewed lunches, a deadline and rush
avoiding the label of being a lush.
Hotel expert with tailored pants
Great Scot, man! I'm one of those ants!

—DA March 1997

Is it the big or little hazards we need to be most wary of as we travel the pathway of life? Here is a verse exploring that question.

Boulder Blindness

We fear and fight life's boulders big
That threaten or block our way
Intimidated by these mighty rigs
That loom to dark our day.

But really should we let those stones
Of giants slow our pace?
Strip living of its proper overtones
And cause wrinkles in our face?

For items large are easily known
We can simply walk around
When they roll or tumble toward our bones
Size shouts a warning sound.

It's those little stones, the gravel
That really takes its toll.
Though "harmless" it can unravel
And doom a lofty goal.

In gravel we can slowly sink,
In gravel we can spin.
In gravel we sideways slink,
In gravel we lose skin.

It's the little lies, the little ties
That block us and beat us down.
Not the boulder of scary size
We fear and dodge around.

Those piddly pebbles under foot
That we crunch and tread above
The daily nags we often put
Aside, **they** cause the shove.

So dodging bullets of cannon size
Is not your worry, man.
It's the "pingers" that will hypnotize,
I warn you that they can.

So look not just up but down
In each day's common tread
Tis little things that break your crown
Not big blows on the head.

—DA October 1996

I love to parallel human behavior with mechanics, be it a cogwheel or a car. This is one of my many poems on such themes.

Alignment

My car it would not hold a course. It veered and pulled like a runaway horse.	My life seemed not to be on course, I wandered, swayed by any force.
It drove unsure on every curve, I'd hit the brakes and it would swerve.	And lost some reason, what to serve, I couldn't stop and lost some nerve.
At any speed 'twas "shimmy, shake," Holding it in line caused hands to ache.	Life summed up to "gimmee—take" A slight setback would make me quake.
I noticed, too, my tire edges bare. No more could I afford the wear.	I was wearing thin, too tired to care To choose a purpose I didn't dare.
I saw a sign—"ALIGNMENT HERE" And so I turned that steering gear.	I felt a sign— "RELIEF HERE— Do what is right and have no fear."
They tightened, leveled, adjusted a screw, squared and directed, added some new.	I discarded habits, all negatives, too, Squared my dealings entirely true.
Balanced and cleared, and did lubricate, It was all done for a minor rate.	I balanced and leveled and cleared any hate The cost here, too, was such a tiny rate.

Straight as an arrow, I traveled now
A little alignment works, somehow.

—DA, Hawaii, June 1995

For some reason I've always been drawn to the "serving" mode (you probably have your pet causes too—some niches of living and doing that gnaw at you to improve or help with). I remember a time in my life when my wife and I had six children of our own, a foster American Indian child, and we were feeding several teenagers working away from home. I was running the Little League team, a youth camp, and was in charge of a large church congregation doing all the marrying, burying, and counseling on things like youth, drugs, and marriage problems. And my wife was often caring for the sick and elderly in our neighborhood and the community. We were really immersed in giving and helping.

One of our nearby neighbors was retired, but still strong, healthy, and energetic. He had a house and a little yard, and for ten hours a day he stayed in and manicured and nitpicked it, while all over the block and everywhere in the community there were homeless, helpless, and suffering people to whom he didn't give a second glance. I asked him to help from time to time and he was always too busy with his place. I watched his life from a distance over the years and one day when I

read his obituary it prompted me to write a
poem, that turned out to be one of my
favorites.

Jones' Plot of Ground

Brother Jones I met one day when calling on him to serve,
Said he, " I haven't time, according to my schedule curve,
You see, my yard," he gestured wide, "tis a glorious plot of ground,
Immaculate to each leaf, why—unequaled in this town."
An' that it was, I looked about, not a blade of grass was wrong,
His plot of ground did indeed reflect, the clipper's trimming tong.
So I left, but returned again one day to request his helping hand,
And always he refused and stayed, on that plot of spotless land.
"I couldn't bear to dwell in an unkempt yard, no matter what the price,
So the only service I will produce is to keep this landscape nice."
As the years of youth went by and into my profession I passed,
Every time I saw his home, he was laboring at this task.
I saw no children or grandchildren ever playing on the velvet lawn,
And never was his wife in view as he labored hours long,
Outside his fence, it mattered not who plead for help to get around.
The only place he showed his face, was to that plot of ground.
Then one day as I drove by, the sprinklers were silent there,
Beside a huge stack of tools, worn out from the years of care.
And across the road in the burial lot, I viewed a fresh new mound
And I knew now that Jones had traded, for another plot of ground.
Much later as I passed the spot marking the final place of Jones,
Twas apparent by the thorns that grew, few cared for his resting bones.
So sad he lays, his soil ungroomed, for eternity must frown,
On that patch of weeds, forever marked, Jones' plot of ground.
—DA 1976

Poetry Can Help Keep Us Going

Championing a cause or accomplishing anything of significance does take effort. Sometimes giving it seems to tax the old body more than we want. I don't know if verse gives any mysterious shot of energy or persistence to the cause of accomplishment in life, but any words that you can line up behind and gain even a morsel of help to march better, write them or grab them!

I've carried these two verses in my notebooks for years, written long ago by one of my verse heroes, Edwin Markham.

> We are all blind until we see, that in the human plan
> Nothing is worth the making, if it does not make the man.
> Who builds these cities glorious
> If man unbuilded goes?
> In vain we build the work unless the builder also grows.

I've also carried two of my own.

Ode to a Good Leader

Bravery, nerve, unselfish thrill
Who's learned to live the great "I will!"

To Been or Not to Been

Someone said of a worn out saint,
"Well, he's just an old has been,
Past his prime, getting quaint
A pile of wrinkled skin."

Sure hope this is said of me
Cause the real mark of never win
Is that person aged the same, you see
Who is just an old **hasn't** been.

—DA May 1996

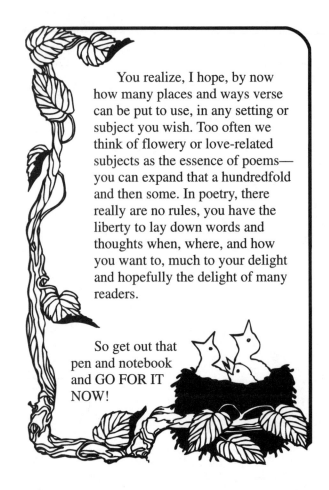

You realize, I hope, by now how many places and ways verse can be put to use, in any setting or subject you wish. Too often we think of flowery or love-related subjects as the essence of poems—you can expand that a hundredfold and then some. In poetry, there really are no rules, you have the liberty to lay down words and thoughts when, where, and how you want to, much to your delight and hopefully the delight of many readers.

So get out that pen and notebook and GO FOR IT NOW!

WHERE YOU CAN LEARN MORE

The following are some good places to learn more about writing poetry, including the technical aspects, as your knowledge and interest in the subject grow. Your librarian can help you find others, including those that may be newly published, or good older books they may have in their collection. The magazines *Writer's Digest* and *The Writer* also often have good articles and columns on poemcrafting.

The Poet's Handbook, by Judson Jerome. Writer's Digest Books, 1980. Detailed instruction in the mechanics and art of writing poetry. Answers the questions most often asked by beginning poets. A very readable and down-to-earth guide.

Poet's Market A directory of places to seek publication for your poetry published annually by Writer's Digest Books. Also contains good how-to information and advice.

Finding What You Didn't Lose: Expressing Your Truth and Creativity Through Poem-Making, by John Fox. G.P. Putnam's Sons, 1995.

Poetry Writing Self Taught, by Pauline D. Robertson. Paramount Publishing, 1998.

Selling Poetry, Verse, & Prose, by Carl Goeller. Doubleday and Company, 1962. A guide to the greeting card and magazine market.

Wishes, Lies, and Dreams: Teaching Children to Write Poetry, by Kenneth Koch.

I Never Told Anybody: Teaching Poetry Writing in a Nursing Home, By Kenneth Koch. Teachers & Writers Collaborative, 1998.

How Does a Poem Mean? by John Ciardi. Houghton Mifflin, 1960.

MY POETRY

CLEANING:

NEW REVISION!

CLUTTER:

MORE MAINTENANCE:

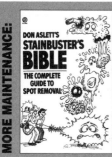

MOTIVATION & BUSINESS:

NEW

PROFESSIONAL CLEANERS:

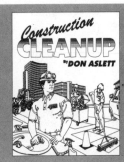